HINTS TO PHILANTHROPISTS

The Development of Industrial Society Series

William Davis

HINTS TO PHILANTHROPISTS

or

A Collective View of Practical Means for Improving the Condition of the Poor and Labouring Classes of Society

IRISH UNIVERSITY PRESS

Shannon   Ireland

First edition Bath 1821

This I U P reprint is a photolithographic facsimile of
the first edition and is unabridged, retaining the
original printer's imprint.

© 1971 Irish University Press Shannon Ireland

All forms of micropublishing
© Irish University Microforms Shannon Ireland

ISBN 0 7165 1564 4

T M MacGlinchey Publisher

Irish University Press Shannon Ireland

PRINTED IN THE REPUBLIC OF IRELAND BY
ROBERT HOGG PRINTER TO IRISH UNIVERSITY PRESS

The Development of Industrial Society Series

This series comprises reprints of contemporary documents and commentaries on the social, political and economic upheavals in nineteenth-century England.

England, as the first industrial nation, was also the first country to experience the tremendous social and cultural impact consequent on the alienation of people in industrialized countries from their rural ancestry. The Industrial Revolution which had begun to intensify in the mid-eighteenth century, spread swiftly from England to Europe and America. Its effects have been far-reaching: the growth of cities with their urgent social and physical problems; greater social mobility; mass education; increasingly complex administration requirements in both local and central government; the growth of democracy and the development of new theories in economics; agricultural reform and the transformation of a way of life.

While it would be pretentious to claim for a series such as this an in-depth coverage of all these aspects of the new society, the works selected range in content from *The Hungry Forties* (1904), a collection of letters by ordinary working people describing their living conditions and the effects of mechanization on their day-to-day lives, to such analytical studies as Leone Levi's *History of British Commerce* (1880) and *Wages and Earnings of the Working Classes* (1885); M. T. Sadler's *The Law of Population* (1830); John Wade's radical documentation of government corruption, *The Extraordinary Black Book* (1831); C. Edward Lester's trenchant social investigation, *The Glory and Shame of England* (1866); and many other influential books and pamphlets.

The editor's intention has been to make available important contemporary accounts, studies and records, written or compiled by men and women of integrity and scholarship whose reactions to the growth of a new kind of society are valid touchstones for today's reader. Each title (and the particular edition used) has been chosen on a twofold basis (1) its intrinsic worth as a record or commentary, and (2) its contribution to the development of an industrial society. It is hoped that this collection will help to increase our understanding of a people and an epoch.

The Editor
Irish University Press

HINTS

TO

PHILANTHROPISTS;

OR,

A COLLECTIVE VIEW

OF

PRACTICAL MEANS

FOR

IMPROVING THE CONDITION OF THE POOR AND LABOURING CLASSES OF SOCIETY.

———◆———

BY WILLIAM DAVIS;

A Member of the " Bath Society for the Investigation and Relief of Occasional Distress, Encouragement of Industry, and Suppression of Vagrants."

———◆———

" Thou shalt love thy neighbour as thyself."
Matt. xxii. 39.

" In proportion as MAN is relieved from the necessity of *labour*, he is debased in the scale of existence."
Quarterly Review, No. xlvi. p. 370.

Bath:

PRINTED BY WOOD, CUNNINGHAM, AND SMITH;
AND SOLD BY J. AND A. ARCH, CORNHILL; LONGMAN AND CO. PATERNOSTER-ROW; AND HARVEY AND DARTON, GRACECHURCH-STREET, LONDON; BINNS AND ROBINSON, BATH; AND OTHER BOOKSELLERS.

———

1821.

PREFATORY LETTER

*To the President, Vice-Presidents, and Committee of
" The Bath Society for the Investigation and Relief
of Occasional Distress, Encouragement of Industry,
and Suppression of Vagrants."*

My respected Friends,

I T is now about four years since you were
pleased to invite me to attend a meeting of your Committee,
convened for the purpose of considering whether some mechanical means might not be adopted in this city for cleansing
chimneys, more consonant with humanity, and the present
refined state of society, than the usual practice of compelling
poor friendless children to sweep them in a way that is
both dangerous and cruel.

It will be recollected, that, subsequently to that meeting,
a Committee was publicly appointed, at the Guildhall of this
city, a considerable sum was raised by subscription, and machines were put into the hands of every master chimney-
sweeper in Bath, with a view of superseding the barbarous
mode of performing these operations by climbing.

After this invitation, you did me the honour to elect me a
member of your respectable Society; and, though I then
stated to you my inability to take my full share of the general
business of your institution, on account of my various engagements of a charitable nature, and other avocations, you were
kind enough to dispense with my regular attendance, and left
me at liberty to meet you whenever it might be convenient
to myself; which liberal conduct, on your part, claims my
grateful acknowledgment.

About that period I had begun to collect information with
regard to the circumstances of the labouring classes of people
in this country, generally, and the most likely means of im-

proving their condition. And now, Gentlemen, permit me to present to you the following "Hints," as the result of these inquiries and observations, in lieu of my personal services, as a member of your Society, which I regret that circumstances prevented me from more frequently affording.

I know no men so capable of judging of the expediency of an undertaking of this nature as yourselves, who continually devote a considerable portion of your time to the Christian duties of visiting the poor in their abodes of want, sickness, and sorrow, and of investigating and relieving their distresses.

Though I am sensible that I possess not the abilities usually deemed requisite for a task of this sort, I hope a humble and sincere desire of rendering even the smallest service to my fellow beings will be accepted as an apology for the defects that may be found in the following pages.

I am persuaded it is the duty of *every man*, whatever his station in life may be, to endeavour, in some way or other, to be useful in society: there is none so insignificant, but that, if possessed of the common faculties of his nature, he may do *some good*.

Society may, properly, be compared to the members of the human body, every member of which depends on the others for assistance. "The eye cannot say to the hand, I have no need of thee: nor again, the head to the feet, I have no need of you:" but if the members of the social body neglect to perform their proper functions, moral disorder must ensue.

The most obvious disorders in the present state of society, or those which appear more particularly to claim the consideration of Christians and philanthropists, may be ranged under two heads, viz. the demoralized condition of the poor and the labouring classes, and the scarcity of the means of rational and useful employment. Perhaps, indeed, it may be said, that the former is, in a great degree, a consequence of the latter: but it will not avail us to attempt to trace the causes that have led to these disorders; whether war and its attendant taxation have principally occasioned the depressed condition of the nation or not; the evils we experience are too obvious to admit any doubt of their existence.

It is plain that something must be out of order in a country which Providence has blessed, of late, with increasing abundance of the good things of this life, and yet in which large numbers of people, however disposed to labour, are unable to procure a sufficiency of the common necessaries of life without the assistance of the parish.

To see multitudes of the labouring classes unable to obtain regular employment, or wages adequate to their necessary wants, and involved in the severest poverty and affliction, is enough to excite our liveliest sympathies. But when men become bereft of all manly spirit and independent principle, and sink into a state of moral and intellectual degradation, abandoning themselves to habits of idleness and vice, which tend to the commission of crime, for which they become victims of the laws; to behold our fellow-beings reduced to a state so abject and deplorable, is surely sufficient to excite in every breast, not devoid of feeling, the deepest commiseration and sorrow.

All thinking men agree that the disorders alluded to imperiously demand the immediate application of some salutary remedy; but they do not all agree as to the kind of means proper to be applied. Some persons may suppose that legislative measures would rectify all our disorders and restore us to a state of health and vigour. But is it reasonable to believe that evils so deeply seated in the nature and constitution of society can be quickly healed by the magic of parliamentary enactments, or by any thing short of individual as well as general exertions?

There seems to be no prospect of an effectual amendment in the state of society, until the members of whom it is composed endeavour, *individually*, to do their duty in that station in which Providence has placed them.

Rank and wealth confer no exemption from individual and social duties, but rather increase the obligation to perform them. We were not placed by our Creator in this world, merely to eat, drink, and sleep, but to be useful one to another; and if the rich and great neglect to fulfil the duties of their stations, fearful indeed will be their responsibility.

Let those in the higher and middle ranks of society begin with setting good examples to their inferiors; for example is more powerful than law. Let the poor be treated as rational beings, as men capable of administering to their own wants; and let their children be educated in a manner suitable to their condition in life, by combining early habits of industry with moral and religious knowledge. Teaching the poor merely to read and write, without these accompaniments, appears to me but a partial good; nay, such acquirements may even be converted into sources of evil.

Let those of riper age be encouraged in practices of industry, sobriety, prudence, and economy, as affording the fairest stock on which religious and virtuous principles may be subsequently engrafted among the labouring classes. Let reasonable inducements be held out by those who occupy superior stations of society for increasing the resources and comforts of these classes : teaching them not only the means of acquiring property from the smallest beginnings, but of prudently laying by part of what they thus earn.

The possession of property will beget in them an interest in the established order of society, and in the preservation of the general welfare. In short, teach the labouring classes to depend alone on their own exertions and good management, for their subsistence, as well as for their comforts, and you will do them a far greater service than in bestowing on them the largest sums, which do not result from their own efforts and good conduct.

These are, I conceive, the only permanent and effectual means (within the reach of Christians and philanthropists) of improving the condition of our Poor, of restoring the country to its former state of prosperity, and of diminishing the weight of our public burthens. As Sir Thos. Bernard has justly observed, " Without these means, workhouses and almshouses, public charities and hospitals, may be erected with increasing and unwearied diligence throughout the land, and yet never keep pace with the progress of indigence and misery."*

Our social as well as religious duties are plain, positive, and indispensable. " Thou shalt love the Lord thy God with " all thy heart, and with all thy soul, and with all thy mind. " This is the first and great commandment. And the second " is like unto it : Thou shalt love thy neighbour as thyself. " On these two commandments hang all the law and the " prophets."†

Love is an *active* principle ; and if it prevailed in our hearts it would undoubtedly shew itself by its fruits. " To love our neighbour as ourselves" must be understood to mean, that we ought to feel a brotherly regard for him, and endeavour to promote his moral and temporal welfare as well as our own. This principle is as truly just as it is beneficent ; gentle, kind, and commiserating ; full of mercy and of good fruits. It is not selfish, but delights in doing good to the utmost of its power. It seeks not to exalt itself by oppressing the poor,

---

* Reports of the " Society for bettering the Condition of the Poor."—Vol. iii. page 29.

† Matt. xxii. 39.

but endeavours to make them virtuous and happy according to their circumstances.

In short, our social duties appear to me to be closely and inseparably allied to those of Christianity; and the proof of our being really Christians must depend on our fulfilling those duties, *individually*, which the necessities of our fellow-creatures appear to call upon us to perform.

On this divine principle, the recommendations contained in the following pages are chiefly founded. To those persons, therefore, who disclaim Christianity as a rule of conduct, our suggestions will appear little better than a waste of time and of labour to both the writer and reader.

After I had begun to turn my attention to the consideration of the state of the poor and the labouring classes, I was favoured with a correspondence with the late Sir Thos. Bernard, to whom I presented a tract which I had published; considering him as a patron and promoter of undertakings of this nature. He was pleased kindly to accept the copy, and gave orders for several hundred more for distribution.*

On the occasion of that correspondence, I took the liberty of suggesting to this eminent philanthropist my opinion, that the public would derive much benefit from the republication, in a smaller shape, of the Reports of the " Society for bettering the Condition of the Poor;" when Sir Thomas presented me, in a friendly manner, with the six entire volumes, besides some odd numbers, of the work, and gave me permission to make such extracts as I thought proper.

Accordingly, the following collection will be found to contain various extracts from the " Reports" of that excellent Society, of which he was an active and distinguished member. Several of these relate to plans acted upon 20 or 30 years since, before machinery had been brought into use so generally as it now is (and, perhaps it may be added, so injuriously to the interests of the labouring classes). I trust, however, that these articles will not prove the less acceptable to the philanthropist, who is desirous of acquiring *practical* information concerning the means already beneficially used for the employment of the poor.

---

* This tract, entitled " FRIENDLY ADVICE," containing maxims of morality and prudence, addressed to persons in humble stations of life, has gone through four editions; and nearly 8000 copies have been printed and circulated, not only in this country, but in several parts of America, and on the continent of Europe.

These pages contain also accounts of several "Schools of Industry," in different parts of England; and of a remarkable establishment at HOFWYL, in SWITZERLAND, for poor Boys, wherein manual employment, united with moral and religious instruction, forms a distinguishing feature of the Institution.

A full account will likewise be found of the operations of an "Association in Dublin for the Suppression of Mendicity," which will be read with interest.

I trust, also, the English reader will derive gratification, as well as practical information, from a copious account which I have extracted from the Essays of Count RUMFORD, of the operations successfully carried on under his auspices, at MUNICH, for the employment of the poor, and the suppression of mendicity, in Bavaria.

For the remainder of the subjects treated of I beg to refer to the Table of Contents; only intimating, that in most of them I desire to appear simply in the character of a *gleaner*, and claim no pretension to originality.

The collection, however, with all its imperfections, is humbly and respectfully presented to the public, as an offering on the altar of Charity, or universal Love; not without a hope that some practical information may be derived from these endeavours to serve the cause of the poor and friendless. And should the smallest benefit result from my labours, may the honour be ascribed alone to the AUTHOR OF ALL GOOD!

I cannot close these prefatory observations which I have the pleasure of addressing to you, my very respected friends, without expressing my most earnest and affectionate desire that those persons of the middle ranks in society, into whose hands this work may come, would seriously consider their moral responsibility as members of the great human family; and endeavour both to know and to perform their social duties in that station in which Providence has placed them. Such persons might become as lights in the world, or as beacons to direct the ignorant and thoughtless into those paths which lead to wisdom and peace; they might also promote the general improvement of the present state of society, which is unhappily become so sadly demoralized.

It is to persons in the middle ranks of life, chiefly, that we are to look for the performance of those active duties which we all owe to our neighbour, or to one another; and as they are the strongest links in the chain of society, which connect the rich and the poor together, their influence and example are of the first consequence to the order, health, and well-being of the social body.

It is principally to the middle classes of society that the poor are accustomed to look for instruction and employment; as being more commonly connected with them by the numerous and useful relations of servants, labourers, artizans, mechanics, and manufacturers: on them, therefore, the lower classes seem more immediately to depend for assistance, and for kind offices, than they do on the absolutely rich, with whom they have but little intercourse.

CHRISTIANITY teaches us to view ourselves in the light of responsible beings; and shows us that we are accountable for the *little* which has been entrusted to our care, as well as for the *much*. Accordingly, we read in the Gospel, that he who had received only *one* talent, and had neglected to improve it, but hid it in the earth, was chargeable with unfaithfulness, inasmuch as he did not occupy therewith according to his ability, and agreeably to the designs of the great Giver.

Let us all, then, whether high or low, rich or poor, endeavour so to occupy and improve the talents or means with which we have been entrusted for the good of society, that when the solemn day of reckoning arrives, we may each receive the welcome sentence of " Well done, good and faithful servant."

With sentiments of respect and esteem,

I remain

Your very sincere Friend,

WILLIAM DAVIS.

Bath; May, 1821.

CONTENTS.

ON LABOUR

OR

USEFUL EMPLOYMENT.

◆◆◆

"In all labour there is profit."—PROV. xiv. 23.
"All things are full of labour."—ECCLES. i. 8.

◆◆◆

PERHAPS it may truly be said, that nothing of a temporal nature is so important to the good order, the comfort, and the very existence of society, as LABOUR or useful employment, whether it be considered in a physical, a moral, or a political point of view. It is the source of our chief enjoyments, and the means by which they are attained: by labour most of our wants are supplied; and without it, nothing valuable or permanent in life can be expected.

1st. Moderate labour is the great preservative of health, and the most powerful antidote against sickness and disease. The labouring man eats his food with a relish to which the idle and the voluptuous are strangers: his rest is sweet, and his sleep undisturbed: and he experiences little care or anxiety so long as he has sufficient employment, and receives for his labour such wages as he is justly entitled to. Even those who have no occasion to work for their subsistence find the necessity of using some exercise, such as riding, walking, &c. as a substitute for labour.

2d. In a moral light, labour is favourable to virtue, and the best preventive of vice. The mind and body of man, being formed by nature for action, require to be constantly employed: those persons, therefore, who are not usefully occupied, are more prone to evil than others. Perhaps a better or a truer reason cannot be assigned for the late alarming increase of crimes, than the general neglect of training the children of the poor to useful labour. The crowded state of our prisons, the number of felons transported or executed, besides the still larger proportion of criminals, who, though guilty, escape punishment, may sorrowfully be traced, for the most part, to a want of proper employment.

3d. In a political light, labour is of the highest importance. It is the source of national and individual wealth, and the vital principle and support of all truly rich and flourishing states. Our food, our clothing, and all the necessaries and comforts of life, are, in this country, primarily obtained by labour. Without culture, indeed, the earth, for the greater part, would yield no corn; without manufactures, the wool of "the flocks of a thousand hills" would yield but poor clothing, and afford but little comfort. Our very enjoyments are so commonly derived from labour, in its more remote results, that they would inevitably cease without it. In short, our condition, without labour, would be like that of savages, who wander about in quest of precarious food, and dwell in holes or caverns of the earth.

Notwithstanding it thus appears that labour is the *greatest good* to society, as well as to individuals, nothing is more true than that it is not generally esteemed. Whether it be that an idea of *pain* is associated with it, or from whatever fatal prejudice the aversion proceeds, certain it is, that it is attended with a sort of natural aversion. But moderate labour is pleasant as well as healthy: if there be evil in it, that evil can only be caused by excess. Nor can we truly say that the abuse of a thing is any good argument against the right use of it. Infinite Wisdom, therefore, to excite us to that which it designed for our good, has ordained that the supply of most of our wants should depend upon labour.

Moreover, we are instructed by the sacred Scriptures that labour was appointed by the beneficent Creator for man, when he was in a state of innocence. He was placed in the garden of Eden, wherein grew "every tree that is pleasant to the sight and good for food;" but in this happy state, in this delightful garden, the labour of man was required, "to dress it and to keep it."

If therefore labour was good for man, while he was in a state of innocence, when the earth produced spontaneously every delicious fruit, "pleasant to the sight and good for food," how much more necessary did it become, after he had transgressed the Divine law, and when his appetites and humours were grown vicious and gross!

On that sorrowful occasion the "Judge of all the earth" passed the following sentence on the first transgressors—a sentence alike marked with pity, with mercy, and with justice: "Cursed is the ground for thy sake! in sorrow shalt thou eat of it all the days of thy life: thorns also and thistles shall it bring forth to thee; and thou shalt eat the herb of the field." "In the sweat of thy face thou shalt eat bread, till thou return unto the ground."—Gen. iii. 17, 19.

With the authority of Scripture then before us, and considering the sentence which the Almighty passed on our first parents as promulgating his gracious purposes towards the whole human race, we are warranted in believing that labour was intended to be the lot, and is the duty, of every son and daughter of Adam; and that a state of idleness was not designed by Divine Wisdom for any of its rational creatures.

But however strong the laws of necessity and duty may be, their force have, unfortunately, been very much weakened in this country by the operation of our Poor Laws. That these were instituted from motives of benevolence cannot be denied; but they have certainly had a most unfavourable effect upon society; and it is evident that, instead of lessening the sum of poverty and misery among the poor, they have greatly increased and multiplied it.

Under these circumstances I shall endeavour to suggest such measures as appear to me likely to counteract the injurious tendency of our Poor Laws; considering man as an independent being, furnished by nature with the ability of ministering to his own wants, and of providing for his own support.

Politically speaking, it becomes the duty of rulers, and others in authority, to promote and encourage labour as much as lies in their power, because the poor in most countries comprise the great mass of the people; and because a matter of such importance to the state as the employment of those who possess no other inheritance than their labour, should not be left to mere chance.

In former times, kings, emperors, and rulers of nations set their subjects honourable examples of labour; and even in the present degenerate age, it is said that every Emperor of China, as soon as he is advanced to the supreme power, is required to give proof of his knowledge of agriculture by ploughing a certain quantity of *land*. But as such rare examples of industry are not to be expected in these days of refinement, it is hoped that the rich, who should be considered as the fathers of the poor, will at least feel themselves bound to promote labour amongst those who possess no other patrimony.

In order to this, it appears that the children of the poor, as soon as they are old enough, should be instructed in various kinds of employment. Whether they be such as promise an immediate pecuniary advantage or not, is of comparatively small importance: the aim should be, to form their youthful limbs to habits of industry, so as to secure permanent profit, in mature age, to themselves and the community.

These habits, as they cannot well be misapplied, are of far greater importance to poor children than their learning to read and write merely. Our daily observation shews us, that unless their minds are properly imbued with moral and religious precepts, a knowledge of reading may be, and often is, productive of a fondness for novels and other pernicious books.

We shall now proceed to consider in what manner every poor child ought to be instructed in labour, or in some useful employment.

Schools of Industry

May be so formed as to combine the useful and healthful employment of children, with their moral and religious instruction, and to make each of these purposes subservient to the other. The tediousness which children feel by being pent up, during a greater part of the day, in large numbers in a close room, where not much more is learnt than to bear confinement, might be agreeably relieved by putting their little hands to some light easy employment during short intervals. And this employment might be occasionally exchanged by the usual instruction of schools: by which means weariness, in such young subjects, would be avoided; and much of that unproductive activity called *play* (which has been generally thought necessary for the health of children) might be superseded, and a variety of light and amusing occupations of industry substituted in its stead. Thus, by judicious management, the little employments of children, instead of being irksome, would become pleasures; and as they advanced in age and strength, their labour would perhaps prove a source of recreation and delight to them, as well as of profit.

In these schools of industry, the most docile and tractable youths might be rewarded or distinguished, so as to excite a spirit of emulation amongst the rest: nothing that has a tendency to oppress ought to be countenanced; but order, variety, and cheerfulness, should be the leading characteristics of the institution.

It might probably be found that perverse and untractable dispositions would yield to a kind and mild treatment more readily than to coercion and rigour.

In country places, and in situations where out-of-door employments could conveniently be adopted, they would be preferable, as being more conducive to health. Boys of seven years old and upwards might be beneficially employed on farms or in gardening, in a variety of ways; of which an example will be given in a subsequent part of this work, drawn from a remarkable Institution at Hofwyl in Switzerland. In this Institution useful employment is so happily blended with habits of order, and with moral and religious instruction, as to have produced a surprising improvement among boys whose propensities had been more than commonly vicious. The children of thieves and beggars have become so reformed under this judicious system, as to be deservedly held up to the country round, as patterns of industry, intelligence, and every other moral virtue.

But we are aware that, in a commercial nation like our own, and in large towns or cities, few opportunities will be likely to occur for instructing poor children in employments out of doors; the occupations of the schools proposed will therefore necessarily be chiefly of the mechanical or manufacturing kinds.

It may not be unnecessary to repeat here, that though the children's labour should not, in the first instance, produce a pecuniary return, this ought to be matter of small consideration, the principal object being to establish early *habits* of industry among them, in the hope that such habits may remain with them thro' life.

Materials produced in our own country, and such as are most easily obtained, are to be preferred; and however plain or homely some of the articles made by the poor may be, yet these, though not eligible to be sent to market, would contribute much to the domestic comfort of their families, or of those of their more destitute neighbours. " In all labour there is profit," saith the wise man; nor does any good come of idleness, but a great deal of evil.

But it will perhaps be said, that the increased quantity of labour resulting from these measures will diminish the value of it, and ultimately prove injurious to the large manufacturer. But are we to be told that we ought rather to let our poor be brought up in idleness, vice, and misery, than to run the risk of injuring the interest of the wealthy and powerful monopolist?

In schools of industry, however, we do not propose to enter into competition with the wealthy manufacturer, aided by the facilities of his machinery. The articles produced in these institutions, or, subsequently, in the dwellings of the poor, are chiefly designed for *usefulness* and *durability:* and if the activity employed in their productions should improve the morals and promote the comfort of the poor, every desirable purpose will be answered. The pecuniary profit may be small;* but we consider every farthing which is added to the value of the home-made article beyond the first cost of the materials, as so much profit, as well morally as politically, since the poor would otherwise be doing nothing, or, what is worse, probably doing evil.

Nets.—Children, when very young, might be taught to make nets: it is easy work; and if they were more numerous, and consequently cheaper, than they now are, they might be more generally introduced into gardens; and a great proportion of our early fruit, such as currants, raspberries, and cherries, now devoured by birds, might be preserved through the summer.

Knitting.—Every poor child, male as well as female, might learn to knit. In the *northern parts* of our island, even boys who keep sheep, or are otherwise employed out of doors, practise knitting. Boys might pass their time pleasantly, as well as usefully, in winter evenings, in knitting stockings.

Wool and *Flax*, those valuable staples of our country, might be

---

* Mr. Firmin formerly observed that " It is much better to lose a *little* by the *industry* than *much* by the *idleness* of the Poor."—Appendix to 4th vol. of the Reports of the " Society for bettering the Condition of the Poor," page 89.

much more generally, and certainly more beneficially worked up by children, or even adults, among the poor, than they now are.

Wool, especially of the coarser kind, may be picked and prepared by children; and though carding requires more strength than they possess, their little hands might be employed in spinning and twisting, and in knitting it into stockings. Formerly, the wives and daughters of labourers and small farmers spun and knit all the stockings necessary for the family, but now-a-days some servants hardly know how to *mend their own stockings!*

Flax grows in many parts of this country, and may be procured in all, in a state fit for spinning thread, making twine, &c. In some districts industrious persons still manufacture their own family linen, which though coarser and less sightly than that produced in large manufactories, is very durable. Flax is generally prepared for dressing by an offensive process of steeping it in pits filled with water, where it remains until it becomes putrescent; and by this process the hard fibres are more easily separated. But a portable machine has lately been invented for bruising and separating the fibres without steeping the flax; which machines are applicable to the use of schools of industry.

Hemp may also be spun, twisted, and made into twine, for ropes, sacking, door-mats, &c. and but little skill is required in manufacturing it.

Basket-making affords a wide scope for employing children and grown persons, in a variety of useful ways, with osiers, rushes, and other materials. This work may be performed even by blind persons; and consequently in winter evenings and in wet weather, in the cottages of the poor, it may be resorted to by persons of all ages, as well for their own use as for sale. In South-Wales they make very neat baskets of a small delicate sort of rush which grows on the sea-coast, called the *sand-rush:* an excellent kind of matting equal to foreign, for passages and rooms, is likewise made of these rushes.

Rush-bottomed Chairs.—A great trade is carried on in this kingdom in chairs, the seats of which are made from bulrushes, both of English and foreign growth. The quantity imported from Holland in the year 1815 is stated at 149,000 bundles, which cost 10,000*l.* of our money. Our rivers abound with bulrushes and flags, would we take the pains to gather them. Rushes are not only used for seats of chairs but for various other purposes, such as matting for rooms, baskets, hassocks, &c. The small common rushes, which grow in abundance in all swampy places, are used by tallow-chandlers for rush-lights, and by basket-makers for door-mats, &c.

Split Straw or *Straw-plat* has been of late years made into hats, bonnets, table-mats, &c.; an employment which affords bread to thousands of our poor. Straw is also worked up into paillasses, beds for poor persons, hassocks, door-mats, beehives, &c.

Toys.—Large sums of money are annually paid to foreigners for the purchase of articles which our own ingenuity and industry ought to supply. How can this be accounted for, otherwise than that our *poor-laws* destroy the motive to exertion in our poor? On visiting the English prisons, while filled with foreigners during the late war, the prisoners were seen busily occupied in making toys, list shoes, and various other articles, by which not only the time, that otherwise would have been a burthen to them, was passed agreeably, but their industry was also rewarded by the *sale* of the articles they had made. Under similar circumstances, is it not probablethat an Englishman would have sat brooding over his troubles, or have beguiled the tedious hours in playing at cards?

Marbles, which are commonly imported, might be made at home. In schools of industry, boys might be taught to make turnery-ware, pegs for the heels of shoes, clothespins for laundresses, vent-pegs, and many other things to render their activity productive.

Every poor boy should be able to mend his shoes, stockings, and other garments. Such practices would keep many out of bad company, and sometimes from the gallows.

Many other means besides the foregoing might doubtless be devised by the benevolent, for instructing and employing the children of the poor. These will be suggested, however, by local circumstances.

If there be but a desire to do good, the means of accomplishing it will be found. The promoting of the *principle* or *habit* of labour among the poor, in all places, cannot be too earnestly or too strongly recommended to those who desire to see the poor happy in the station appointed for them by nature and by Providence.

Without useful employment, neither virtue nor happiness will be found among the lower classes of our fellow beings.

Having thus made a few general observations on the duty as well as the necessity of labour, and on the advantages to be derived to society from the employment of the children of the poor, (more especially from training them to habits of industry,) I shall now proceed to the detail of several practical plans of labour, blended with moral instruction, that have already been put in execution with the best effects in different parts of the country. I consider that these Institutions exhibit the most salutary methods of educating the poor; and it is obvious that while they |have produced an increase of individual virtue and happiness among the lower orders, they have also greatly tended to reduce the public burthens wherever they have been established. As *facts* too have always a stronger claim to attention than the most plausible *theories,* they appear to be particularly entitled to consideration, from their good effects having been proved during a period before the modern system of machinery had spread its demoralizing influence among the manufacturing classes.

Employment of Poor Children at Birmingham.

In the 123d Report of the "Society for bettering the Condition of the Poor," vol. iv. p. 203, an interesting account is given of the advantages that had been derived at BIRMINGHAM from a plan of separating the children in the PARISH WORKHOUSE from those depraved and incorrigible persons who too frequently form the inmates of such habitations. These children, many of whom were either illegitimate or deserted by their parents, had, before the adoption of this plan, been occasionally placed out with nurses in the neighbouring villages. The expense and inconvenience, however, of this mode of disposing of them had suggested the formation of a separate establishment.

A large building, about a mile from the town, was engaged, and designated the "Asylum." A matron was appointed, who, with a school master and mistress and one female servant, formed the household. The girls were to be employed in assisting to clean the rooms, make the beds, &c.; employments which, while they promote economy, tend to preserve health and establish habits of domestic usefulness. They were also to be taught to read, and to be employed in knitting, needle-work, &c. for the house, the parish workhouse, and respectable families; and they have gained such credit from their work, that more has been sent them than they have been able to execute. Besides this, they were to be employed in platting straw for bonnets and hats, which would turn to a good account.

In this Asylum a trial has been made of employing forty of the boys, under a pin-maker, in heading pins, and sticking them in papers in rows; which trial having proved successful, the number of boys so occupied has been doubled. The Overseers and Guardians also were so well satisfied, that the pin-shop has been since considerably enlarged.

"Besides the benefit accruing to the Institution from their labour, the children themselves acquire early *habits* of industry and subordination, to which before they were entire strangers; for previously to this attempt to civilize these forlorn and unhappy creatures (most of whom had never known the reciprocal endearments and powerful operation of parental or filial affection), their rude and savage manners, and disregard of authority, rendered them so untractable and turbulent, as for some time to baffle every effort of the COMMITTEE to correct them.

"The first expedient that contributed at all to this object was the placing of them in classes, and conducting them in order round the governor, in the play-gound, several times a-day; when he had an opportunity of marking their individual conduct, of correcting the disorderly, and of applauding the tractable. This was followed by placing them in order at meals, and by every other measure that occured, for impressing upon them ideas and habits of order and regularity.

" The good effects of these measures became daily more and more apparent; and these children are now become as orderly and as decent as such a number of children under one roof could ever have been expected to become.

" They have a regular Sunday service, which is decently performed by a respectable young man, a clerk in the workhouse, who concludes with reading a sermon. On this service the whole family attends, with much order and propriety.

" The children have meat three times a week: they have also soup, puddings, rice, milk, bread, cheese, and beer; and these the best of their kind. The medical gentlemen, who are employed for the workhouse, attend weekly in succession, and two physiciane of the town have benevolently given their services, when called upon.

" The COMMITTEE, five in number, meet once a week at the ASYLUM, for the regulation of the accounts, and for the general superintendance of the whole. Each takes his department in providing the different supplies; making himself responsible for the quality, quantity, and terms, on which the articles are purchased. Thus the children are better kept, and with more economy, than on any preceding plan.

" The great object of this Institution is eventually to place these children in society, with the advantage of better habits and propensities, than they would have obtained without some such preparative education. And such has been the effect of the means applied, that they, who had been once the pest and dread of housekeepers and manufacturers, are now sought for with avidity, as orderly and useful servants; and have every opportunity afforded them of enjoying a comfortable and permanent subsistence.

" These are certainly great advantages, especially as they have been obtained, not only without cost, but have been attended with the saving to the parish of a sum so considerable as THREE THOUSAND POUNDS, in the space of seven years."

Thus the parish has not only made a saving of more than 400*l.* a year (on an average of seven years), but has sent out the poor children with the means and ability of maintaining themselves; has diminished the profligacy, and improved the habits and industry of their neighbourhood; and has had the gratification of observing a gradual and uninterrupted progress in habits of prudence, morality, and religion, in a class of young persons who in many other parishes are daily proceeding from idleness and disorder to the commission of crime.

Statement of Savings.

FIRST YEAR.

The average number of Children 248, if put out to nurse, would have cost the parish, at 2s. each per week 1289 12 0

Saving to the Parish.

Their maintenance, including rent, fire, wages, &c. at the Asylum, at 1s. 4½d. each per week, cost .. .... 884 2 0—405 10 0

SECOND YEAR.

The average number of children 290, if at nurse, would cost, at 2s. each, per week 1508 0 0

Their maintenance, at 1s. 4¼d. each per week, cost .... 1021 8 5—486 11 7

THIRD YEAR.

Average number 269, at 2s. each per week 1748 10 0

Their maintenance, at 1s. 10d. each per week .... 1283 1 4—465 8 8

FOURTH YEAR.

Average number 281, would have cost, at 3s. each per week 2191 16 0

Maintenance, at 2s. 1½d. each per week 1555 14 6—636 1 6

FIFTH YEAR.

Average number 250, at 2s. 9d. each per week 1787 10 0

Maintenance, at 2s. 4¼d. each per week 1532 1 4—255 8 8

SIXTH YEAR.

Average number 200, at 2s. 9d. each per week 1430 0 0

Maintenance, at 2s. 2½d. each per week 1153 10 8—276 9 4

SEVENTH YEAR.

Average number 235, at 2s. 9d. each per week 1680 5 0

Maintenance, at 1s. 11½d. each per week 1196 10 10—483 14 2

£3009 3 11

This account is dated 5th January, 1805, and we understand the Institution still continues to prosper.

Should it here be objected that every town has not the advantage of a pin-manufactory, to employ poor children, like that at Birmingham, we grant it; but we believe there are few or no towns in the kingdom, in which some employment may not be found, either in wool, flax, hemp, or cotton; or in making of baskets, nets, mats, list shoes, carpetting, chair-bottoms, or some other useful articles, such as we have suggested in our chapter entitled " Schools of Industry."

Cheltenham School of Industry for Girls, to be educated as Under-Servants.

Patronized by the late Queen.

" This Charity was instituted with a view to promote *religion* and *industry* among the FEMALE POOR, by impressing their minds early with a just sense of the importance of both, to their present as well as future happiness; and to place them more effectually beyond the necessity of being tempted to swerve from rectitude, by enabling them, in various ways, to earn an honest livelihood.

" Besides baking, milking, washing, ironing, and every kind of household work, they are taught to spin wool, flax, and hemp; to knit, to sew, to plat whole straw for baskets, and to cut out and make clothing, which is afterwards sold to the poor at reduced prices. The School also gives, under certain restrictions, a stated price for work to any girls or young women who apply for it, and who might otherwise, perhaps, for want of employment, fall victims to idleness and vice.

" It has been asked, why the Cheltenham Charity so particularly points out a course of education for *under-servants*, and why *writing* is not taught in the School? The complaint in all parts of England is not the want of *upper* female-servants, but of hard-working *under*-servants, who will quietly and properly do *all sorts* of household business. To restore, therefore, this useful class of servants to Society, appeared desirable; and as the children admitted to this charity are the offspring of poor labourers and mechanics, they seem, with very few exceptions, peculiarly calculated to fill those humble, but not less happy stations. For this purpose, as *early* impressions and habits have a great influence on the future conduct in life, every thing around them is suited to the sphere in which they are intended hereafter to move, as servants, wives, or daughters. And on leaving the Institution, they may be expected to carry with them the remembrance of what for six years constituted their chief happiness and comfort—habitual attention to religious duties, to order, to neatness, and cleanliness, with the power of earning, in various ways, an honest livelihood.

" *Writing* is not taught, because experience has shewn it to be the source of the very evil, for the counteracting of which the Cheltenham School was planned. As soon as a pen is put into the hands of that class of children of which the Charity consists, the ignorant parents attach to it an idea of *scholarship** and *capability,*

---

* It is lamentably obvious that even the ability to read, when unaccompanied with moral and religious instruction, has often proved an evil, instead of a good, to female servants, who thereby get access to novels, and other mischievous publications, by which their morals become corrupted.

which, in their opinion, entitles their children to services of less labour, and higher wages."

PLAN.

The Shcool is divided into Three Classes.

FIRST CLASS consists of Twelve Girls on the Fund.
SECOND CLASS consists of Twelve ditto paid for by their **Parents.**
THIRD CLASS consists of Girls put in by Subscribers.

First Class.—Twelve Girls, children of the most deserving parishioners, from 11 to 12 years old, selected from among those who bore the best characters in the Sunday-Schools (two being nominated by the Patroness), are admitted on the fund every three years, and clothed in a plain substantial uniform dress.

Second Class.—Twelve Girls, from 10 to 11 years old, selected and chosen as above, are admitted on their parents' paying two-pence per week for their schooling. They have the same advantages as the " fund " girls in respect to clothing, and also remain three years in this class; at the end of which time they are removed into the first class for three years more, which makes the whole time of their schooling six years. If any circumstance should occasion the removal of a girl of the first class, before the expiration of the stated time, her place may be filled up by one out of the second class, according to the number of *merit-tickets* the candidate has obtained for good conduct during the year. The girl to be chosen by a Committee of Subscribers.

It is believed that making the parents pay something for the schooling of their children will be a means of exciting them to industry, as so many advantages will accrue to them from it.

Third Class.—Girls put in by Subscribers.—Every Annual Subscriber of one guinea, on applying to the Trustees, is entitled to send a girl, not under seven years old, to the School. And each Subscriber of ten shillings and sixpence is entitled to purchase clothing at the reduced price to the amount of six shillings.

INSTRUCTION.—The Instruction of the Children in this School is nearly the same as in other Charity-Schools, except with respect to writing, which is excluded; and as our limits will not allow us to go into any unnecessary details, we shall proceed to the

REGULATIONS OF THE SERVANTS' STATIONS.

The *Work-Girl* takes care of the work-baskets, thread-papers, pin-cushions, all the plain work, and the work-bags; and observes that the thimbles and scissars are in their proper places: she has also the care of the knitting, the sheaths, pins, &c.; and gives out the work, and takes it away.

The *Book-Girl* takes care of the books, and places them according to their number; she gives them out, and takes them in, beginning at the highest number. She also takes care of the spools, rocks, and spindles, the spinning-wheels and reels, the straw-platting, &c. and gives them out.

The *Bonnet-Girl* takes and gives out the bonnets, sees that the pattens and cloaks are placed according to number and order, and regularly sweeps the play-ground, or the place where the children play, after play-hours.

The *Laundry-Maid* washes the girls' tippets, caps, and aprons, and the house-linen on Thursdays, and irons on Fridays.

The *Upper-Maid* lays the cloth for dinner, washes the plates, mugs, &c.; attends on the *Matron* at dinner and tea; washes the tea-things and the glass; takes care of the house-linen, and of the children's clothing: she gives it out on Saturday, and sees that it is all returned, and properly placed in the store-room on the Monday following. She combs and washes the girls on Mondays and Thursdays; and when she has done her own work, she assists in dusting the house, if wanted; she has also the care of the stores for feeding the children.

The *House-Maid*, whilst she continues in office, sleeps at the school, dusts the school-room and house every morning, sweeps the school every day after dinner, and rubs and sweeps it every evening after school-hours. She scours the house, the stairs, and clothing-room on Tuesdays and Saturdays; sweeps the walls on Wednesdays; cleans the irons and grates on Thursdays, and wipes them daily: she rubs the tables, chairs, drawers, and presses on Thursdays; and helps to wash and comb the girls.

The *Kitchen-Maid* lights the fires, dresses the Matron's dinner, cleans the saucepans and kettles every day, helps to wash the plates and dishes, cleans the dressers and deal tables every Tuesday; scours the brasses, &c. on Wednesdays; cleans the children's knives and forks and the *medals* on Fridays, also the spoons, &c.: she likewise cleans the outhouses every day, and keeps all in order in the kitchen.

The House-Maid and Kitchen-Maid clean the shoes on Mondays.

" Let each domestic have her proper place,
" And know that *order* is the greatest grace."*

Visiter's Card.—A printed card is put into the hands of ladies who come to see the school; describing the official duties of the several girls, and the situations in which the work, clothing, and other articles, are to be found. They are requested to inspect these, and observe whether well or ill done, and to bestow praise

---

* We have seen written in a conspicuous place, in some schools, "The order of this School is, *a place for every thing, and every thing in its place.*"

or censure accordingly as the children appear to deserve it. These modes of investigation prove a means of keeping them alive to a sense of their duties.

Every girl has a written list of the things under her care, for which she is accountable; and she is obliged to make good the deficiency, if there be any, when she delivers up her charge to the next.

Tickets of Merit are given to the most deserving girls. One hundred white tickets entitle the possessor of them to a prize. The number of prizes to be obtained in six years are fifteen; their value, all together, amounts to 3*l*. 7*s*. 6*d*. which sum is given to the girl entitled thereto in books, clothes, and money, when she goes to service, or when she leaves the school with the approbation of the Committee. These tickets are considered the highest rewards that can be conferred on the girls who distinguish themselves by strict attention to their religious duties, or to cleanliness, or who are the "best servants," the " best workers" in the different employments, the " best readers," the " most industrious," the " best tempered," the "most kind to their schoolfellows," the " best monitors," &c. &c.

The *Black Book* (which is not shewn) has a page appropriated to each girl with columns for the following faults, viz. lying, swearing, stealing or pilfering, cruelty, revenge, insolence, &c. &c.

A number of appropriate rules for the conduct of the children, besides instruction and advice to their parents, are contained in the pamphlet from which this account is extracted (to be had at the School, price two shillings), the whole of which our limits will not allow us to insert here.

An acquaintance with the following *Regulations* may, however, prove useful, where similar institutions are proposed to be formed.

The children whose parents reside in the town of Cheltenham, or within a given distance of it, are clothed, boarded, and educated for ten pounds a-year. Those from a greater distance are clothed, boarded, and educated at twelve pounds per year. They must be recommended by a subscriber, or member of the Committee; and the parents must apply to the *Trustees* for the admission of their children, and give security to them for the half-yearly payments from the day of admission.

None can be admitted who have not previously undergone vaccination, or had the small-pox.

The parents or friends of the children engage to remove them on their being seized with any catching or infectious disorder; and they engage to be answerable for funeral expenses in case of death, and for expenses incurred by any illness of more than a month's duration.

No child who has not been entered into the first and second classes, nor worn the uniform, nor made one of the 24 children originally admitted, can be received as a boarder.

Although this Institution educates girls for servants, it does not bind itself to procure places for them; but they will be entitled to clothes and recommendations, on their friends' providing them with situations, at the end of the six years.

The girls are not sent to service until they are seventeen; when each of them receives the following books, viz. a Bible; a Prayer-Book; a Companion to the Altar; the Pious Parishioner; Young Woman's Monitor; the Servant's Friend, by Mrs. Trimmer; Address to Children of Sunday-Schools, by Major Brooke; Mary Wood, or the Danger of False Excuses; and Mrs. Trimmer's Charity-School Spelling-Book, Part 2d.

EMPLOYMENT.—The several kinds of work in which the girls are employed have been described in the second paragraph of this chapter: but the employment of young women generally cannot be too earnestly recommended; it is absolutely a national concern, and the interest of the whole community. It is well known that the morals of women, sooner or later, influence those of men. Idleness is the corrupter of female virtue in the lower, as well as in the higher, classes of society; and the want of employment for young women, among the poor, leads them into the path of destruction. A proper situation cannot always be found for every young woman in want of one; and if she goes to service, it may probably be only for a few months; she returns, perhaps in winter, when there is nothing for her to do: she must then add to her father's expense, and her mother's care, without the possibility of becoming useful to them. If such a young person could obtain the loan of a spinning-wheel, and have some wool or flax to spin, she would be kept out of mischief, and earn some part, at least, if not all of her subsistence, as long as there was a necessity for her to remain under the roof of her parents. More need not be said, as it is an incontrovertible fact, that the miseries and depravity of most women originate in want of employment.

Were it possible to reduce to practice the following hints, the distresses of the poor would be greatly alleviated. Every parish should have linen and woollen spun, during the four winter months, when there is no work to be done in the fields, these materials should be manufactured for the poor of that parish, *and that parish only.*

Every parish should have a HOUSE OF INDUSTRY, which would also serve as a warehouse for goods manufactured by the poor, and a depôt for utensils, such as spinning-wheels, looms, &c. Articles of food, such as wheat, barley, and flour, as well as bread, should be laid in respectively on the best terms, and, with the goods manufactured, sold to the poor during winter, at a reduced price, for ready money. In like manner, fuel, sold to the poor from a public magazine, at a rate within their means of purchase, would not only add infinitely to their comfort and health, but probably prove a means of curing habits of dishonesty in some, and of preventing them in others; as the early practice of breaking hedges and stealing wood often opens a door to greater depredations, and leads the infant thief, at a maturer age, to the gallows.*

SKETCH OF A PLAN FOR A SCHOOL OF
INDUSTRY FOR BOYS.

(Extracted from the Cheltenham Pamphlet.)

THE boys are to be taken out of Sunday-Schools at from ten to twelve years of age, and to receive an education in this Institution for two or more years; being intended for farmers' or other servants: they are to be taught weaving and basket-making, and to make and mend shoes. Looms to be kept in the house for weaving coarse cloth or sheeting, which is to be sold to the poor at a reduced price. The boys may also make ropes, twine, and sacking; work in the garden; and assist old men in hedging and ditching, or in mending the roads occasionally; under the direction and controul of the Charity.

After the first year, a boy may be paid a certain price for his labour, the profits of which should go to his parents.

All the persons in the Institution to assemble at 9 o'clock in the morning, after breakfast is over, to prayers; to dine at 12 (either bringing their dinners or paying two-pence), and to return to the school at 2 o'clock. Evening prayers to be read at 6 in summer, and at 4 in winter; by which time all the boys who are out at work are to return to the school. After prayers, ten boys, or any given number, may write; the same number may read; others may spell or learn by heart; others cypher: and they may take, by turns, for six weeks at a time, the offices of assistant and monitor. Assistants are to teach the different classes, and monitors to attend to the conduct of the boys.

The servitors to clean the knives and shoes, attend to keeping all places clean and neat, lay the cloth, fetch the dinner, &c. &c.

---

* This benevolent recommendation, contained in the Cheltenham pamphlet, has for the most part been adopted at DORKING, where a PROVIDENT INSTITUTION was happily established three years since, in which the poor, by depositing a small sum weekly, during the eight most productive months, receive, in the four unproductive months of winter, bread, flour, and fuel, according to the number contained in their families, at reduced prices: the deficiency from such sale at reduced prices being made up by donations and subscriptions from the wealthier inhabitants.

This admirable Institution has exceeded the highest expectation of its benevolent founders by exciting a spirit of industry and forethought among the poor; many have been made comfortable, and prevented from becoming chargeable to the parish, by its means.

The religious instruction, spelling and reading, to be taught according to Dr. BELL's plan. It is also proposed that a lecture, or, more properly speaking, a plain, simple, well established and sanctioned explanation of the Church Catechism and Liturgy, be given every Friday evening by the Curate or Clergyman of the parish, at which the attendance of all the boys should be strictly required.

Prizes to be given for exemplary attention to religious duties, and other good conduct. The behaviour of the boys to be regularly noticed in a book, and the most deserving to be rewarded, at the end of two years, with a Bible, and a sum not exceeding one guinea in money.

The Master and Mistress of this Institution should be man and wife; the latter may have the care of the girls' department: they should be persons of good education, and their salaries should be liberal': coals, candles, and vegetables should be allowed them.

** *It is much to be desired that* INSTITUTIONS, *on plans similar to the foregoing, were generally established throughout the country.*

The same interesting pamphlet suggests the following

"RULES FOR THE MANAGEMENT OF A PARISH MANUFACTORY."

That the spinning of flax and wool continue for four months only every year; namely, from the first week in November to the end of the first week in March.

That none but the poor of the parish be employed; nor, among them, any who have regular employment from manufacturers in the neighbourhood.

That the work be given out and paid for, once a week, by the superintendant, at the market-house [or house of industry]; and that wheels be then lent to those who have not any of their own.

That a committee of six gentlemen, the treasurer and overseers of the parish for the time being, superintend this manufactory; and meet, for the inspection of accounts and other business relative to it, once a month.

That the parish be divided into districts; each gentleman of the committee undertaking the inspection of his own district, and, at the meeting in October, giving an account of the statement of the poor in it.

That at the October meeting orders be given for the purchase of such materials as are necessary to carry on the manufactory; and that the quantity and quality of the goods to be manufactured be then determined.

That the money be placed in the hands of bankers, and drawn out by the treasurer and one of the committee.

That, at a meeting at the close of the manufacturing season, an account be taken of the goods on hand; of the flax, wool, and oil left, and also of the wheels, turns, cards, and other utensils deposited at the market-house; and of such repairs as may be necessary for the same.

That the superintendant give an account to the overseers, at each monthly meeting, of the persons employed, and of the sums they have earned.

That the superintendant receive four shillings a week for his services.

That such women, girls, or boys, as are unacquainted with spinning, and are desirous to learn, be taught at the poor-house.

⁎ *A Plan for a* PARISH BANK *for labourers succeeds to this, somewhat similar to that of the " Dorking Provident Institution," before alluded to.*

EXTRACT FROM AN ACCOUNT OF

A Spinning-School at Oakham, in the county of Rutland:

Patronized by the Earl of Winchelsea.

RULES.

1st. All inhabitants of the parish shall be admitted.

2d. No persons shall receive relief from the parish upon account of their families, who refuse to send their children to the School; unless they can prove, to the satisfaction of the Overseers, that they can employ them to more advantage elsewhere.

3d. Every person who desires it shall be instructed, *gratis*, in spinning jersey and linen, and in knitting: they who choose it, in reading; and they who can bring work with them, in sewing.

4th. The hours of work shall be from eight to one, and from two to seven; the hour from one to two being allowed for dinner and rest. No work after dinner on Saturdays.

5th. A dinner shall be provided for those who choose to dine at the School on the working-days; for which they shall pay each 6d. per week.

6th. In case of illness, the dinner shall be sent for to their homes.

7th. The portions, if the dinner is sent out, shall be as follow:

One pint and a half of pease porridge.

Ditto .... of rice milk.

Ditto .... of rice broth.

One pound and a half of potatoe pudding.

Those who dine at the School shall have as much as they choose to eat, and a quarter of a pound of bread each; except on the pudding and rice milk days, when no bread is allowed.

8th. The whole of the earnings shall *belong to the children.*

OBSERVATIONS.

A Spinning-School had been established at OAKHAM in 1787; but until the arrangement just described took place the children used to go home to their dinners, which was attended with great inconvenience in wet and bad weather, and with loss of time also. When the weather was very bad they seldom returned after dinner, and sometimes did not attend at all.

In order to establish the present system, the dinners were given *gratis,* for the first fortnight, and the parents were invited to taste them: they were afterwards informed that the children of those who approved of the plan *might* dine there, upon their paying *sixpence a week* each; and that those whose parents preferred their dining at home might continue to do so. The parents all preferred their dining at the school; and the whole number, which now amounts to between sixty and seventy, pay their money and dine there. They do more work weekly by these means, and get a much better dinner than they could at home. Several children attend there, whose parents do not receive parochial relief.

By purchasing the different articles on wholesale terms, by the use of barley bread (which is customary at that place), and by means of a "Rumford" copper, the expense of the dinners and fuel has never exceeded the sixpence per head.

The methods of preparing the pease porridge and pudding are taken from COUNT RUMFORD's book, with a few alterations, which make them rather more expensive, but certainly better.

I conceive that the success which has hitherto attended this plan, is owing to its having been left to the *option* of the parents, whether their children should dine there or not.—16th Mar. 1767.

EXTRACT FROM AN ACCOUNT OF

A School of Industry for Children, at Lewisham, in Kent:

By John Forster, Esq.

" In April, 1796, a Meeting of the inhabitants of Lewisham was called, for the purpose of establishing a *School of Industry*, for the Children of that parish. The Subscribers came to a resolution to prepare accommodations for the reception of 60 children; and the house was opened on the 30th of May, 1796.

The children are admitted on the recommendation of subscribers, and by an order of the committee. In summer, the school is open from six o'clock in the morning till six at night; and in winter, during the hours of daylight: but the children have usually finished their task by two o'clock; they then go away, unless, which is the case with some of them, they *prefer* to work additional hours on *their own account*. They receive two meals a day, a breakfast and a dinner; one hour being allowed at dinner, and half an hour at breakfast. They are employed in *spinning, winding*, and *knitting*, and *one boy in weaving*. The present weaver is an active boy, not 10 years of age: his predecessor had been employed but a very little time, before he had an offer of a permanent engagement at a cotton-mill. In rotation they all receive lessons in reading.

The children's weekly maintenance is estimated at 1s. 6d. per head; and where they earn more in any week, (as some do 6d. and some 1s. a week) they are paid, and carry home the surplus. One little boy (who came from the workhouse with a bad character, but who now possesses a very good one) earns not less than an extra shilling a week: he has, during the last month, put into the master's hands, in trust for him, the sum of 5s. In the case of the parish children, who are maintained entirely at the parish expense, there is as yet no certain allowance given them; but they are rewarded according to their industry and good behaviour. It is however in contemplation to make them a fixed allowance; probably *a sixth part of their earnings.*

Spinning-wheels are lent, and materials are supplied, to any of the adult inhabitants of the parish, who wish to have employment at their own homes; and their work is paid for upon delivery. A suit of clothes, made of the cloth and camlet of their own manufactory, is yearly given to each of the children who attend the school, as a reward for their good behaviour, and in order to enable them to appear decently and regularly at church on Sundays.

In the infancy of any manufacture, there is necessarily a *loss* resulting from the *waste* of raw materials. In the present instance, it must be admitted that very little profit accrued from the labour of the children during the first six months: but during the next half-year the profit *gradually increased;* and it advanced so much, that at the end of the year, on the 30th of May, 1797, the net profit of the manufactory amounted to 55*l.* That profit may be fairly estimated at 100*l.* a year in future. The School of Industry now supplies the parish workhouse with most of their articles of clothing: besides which, a stock of knitted stockings, and of camlets and worsteds, is kept in the warehouse, to be sold by wholesale and retail. The demand for them has been gradually increasing; and the inhabitants have found their advantage in the purchase of them.

The weekly expense of the family, upon an average, is 3*d.* a head per day; including the 20 parish children and the master and mistress and their two children, who have their three meals a day and lodge in the house. For each of the parish children the establishment is allowed the sum of 3*s.* a week, which is near 50*l.* a year less than the expense of merely feeding them in the workhouse during the preceding year.

The following is a pretty correct estimate of the expenses and receipts of the establishment.

PAYMENTS.

	£.	s.
To the maintenance of the family, clothing, &c.	250	0
To the wages of the Master & Mistress, at 10s. per week	26	0
To the wages of the Schoolmistress, who teaches the children to read	3	0
To the rent of the house, and of a wooden building behind	13	0
To Insurance	1	0
To Mr. Hall, the manager, who does not live in the house, but who attends occasionally, purchases the provisions and materials for the work, and provides a sale for the articles of manufacture ..	30	0
To incidents, gratuity to the Secretary, &c.	26	10
	£350	0

RECEIPTS.

	£.	s.
From parish rents appropriated to the Institution	60	0
From allowance for 20 parish children, at 3s. a week each	156	0
From profits of the manufactory per annum, supposed	100	0
From deficiency in the infancy of the establishment, to be made good by subscriptions	34	0
	£350	0

There are 48 persons, including the master and mistress and their two children, who breakfast and dine regularly in the house: the table of diet, and quantities of provision allowed, which are quite as much as they wish, are as follows:

MONDAY.—*Breakfast*. Rice milk: made of 4lb. of rice, 1lb. of flour, 1lb. of sugar, and 4 quarts of milk.—*Dinner*. Twenty pounds of beef, and a peck of potatoes, with 17lb. of bread.

TUESDAY.—*Breakfast*. Broth and 13lb. of bread.—*Dinner*. Boiled rice: consisting of 15lb. of rice, 1½lb. of sugar, and 3 quarts of milk,

WEDNESDAY.—Same as Monday.

THURSDAY.—Same as Tuesday.

FRIDAY.—*Breakfast*. Gruel: made of 2 quarts of oatmeal, with the allowance of 1lb. of butter, 11lb. of bread, and 4 oz. of salt.—*Dinner*. Beef-stew: consisting of 22lb. of shins of beef, and a peck of potatoes, with 17lb. of bread.

SATURDAY.—Same as Tuesday and Thursday.

The workhouse children and the master's family (in all 24) have, for their Sunday's breakfast, gruel, made of 1 quart of oatmeal, with the allowance of half a pound of butter, 8lb. 10oz. of bread, and 4oz. of salt:—for dinner, 12lbs. of beef, half a peck of potatoes, 5lb. 5oz. of bread, 8oz. of salt, and 3 quarts of beer:—for supper on Sunday, 6lb. 8oz. of bread, ½lb. of cheese, and 2 quarts of beer. They have the same supper on the other days of the week, with a small additional allowance of bread, of which they seem to require more on week-days than on Sundays. The price of the beef is 3s. a stone, or 4½d. per pound; of the two shins of beef (weight per average, including bone, 22lb.) 2s. 6d.; of potatoes, 20d. a bushel; of their bread, which is good seconds, 7½d. the quartern loaf, or rather more than 1½d. a pound.

By the preceding bill of fare it will appear, that the cheap article of *rice* now forms a very considerable proportion of the children's diet. The use of it has been gradually increasing, partly in consequence of their having acquired a greater fondness for it than for other food, and partly because it has been observed to possess nutritive and wholesome qualities. Its average increase, on being boiled in mere water, has been found to be fourfold; with the addition of milk it is much more.—The good health which the children uniformly enjoy has been remarkable: several of them, who were weak and sickly at their admission, have since that period become healthy and vigorous; to which their new habits of cleanliness and regularity, and the exercise of spinning by hand-wheels in an airy apartment, as well as their diet, may probably have conduced. The improvement in their morals and behaviour has been equally satisfactory to the promoters of the Institution. It is found, that, in proportion as the children become skilful and useful, their parents and friends learning their value, become desirous of withdrawing them, because they can employ them to more advantage. This has already been the case with many; and such an event has generally happened in the course of 8 months after they have been received into the school. The habits of order and industry, which the children acquire at this school, render them so desirable as apprentices, that, though there was a difficulty formerly in finding situations in private families for any *parish* children, because *they came out of a work-house*, yet they are *now sought after*, and the parish is relieved from the expense of their maintenance at a much earlier age than if they had been kept in the workhouse.

One other very great advantage resulting from this establishment, and from its necessary connexion with the poor of the parish, is, that the gentlemen who have interested themselves in its success, have thereby been induced to take a very active part in the management of the poor; and one of them, ROBERT SAUNDERS, Esq; is now serving the office of overseer for his second year. It is obvious that this Institution is of incalculable benefit to the poor, and it causes a saving to the parish of scarcely less than 500*l.* a year.

OBSERVATIONS.

The preceding account will shew how much may, at a very small expense, be effected by a judicious and spirited adoption of one of the measures directed by the statute 43d Elizabeth. It is almost needless to enumerate the effects which have been necessarily produced upon the *morals,* the *cleanliness,* and the *health* of the children. They are habituated to industry, instructed in reading, accustomed to a regular attendance on divine service, are bred up in the knowledge and practice of obedience and reverence to their Creator, and are of that utility which he has enjoined as a duty to their fellow-creatures. Besides the advantages of separating the children from the contagion of those dissolute and profligate characters which are to be found in all workhouses, the maintaining of them at a lesser expense, and the educating of them in the habits of industry and virtue, very great relief is given by these means to the parent poor of the parish. They are eased of the burden of maintaining so many of their children at home, and the mothers obtain profitable employment; a relief that has a just and honourable tendency to reduce the poor's rates. Establishments like that at Lewisham have also the merit of preventing the little pilfering habits of the infant poor, which form the source of so many little vices and crimes in society; of preserving them from idleness and bad examples; and of training them in virtuous and industrious habits, so as to make them blessings to their parents, and useful and valuable members of society."—22d *February,* 1798.

EXTRACT FROM AN ACCOUNT OF

A School of Industry for Sixty Girls, at Bamburgh Castle:

By the Rev. R. G. Bowyer.

" Sixty poor girls, elected from the township and neighbour-hood of Bamburgh, in the county of Northumberland, are taught to spin jersey and flax, to knit, to sew, and to mark; and are also instructed in religion, psalmody, reading, writing, and the ele-mentary parts of arithmetic. None are admitted under the age of five years. The twelve youngest are taught reading and knitting only; the remainder are divided into two sets of 24 each: when the school is complete, the sets are alternately employed, for a week at a time, in two rooms, and each set superintended by a separate mistress.

The lower room is about forty feet long, twenty broad, and and above twenty high. This is wholly appropriated to spinning. The jersey spinners occupy the floor with twelve wheels and a large reel; and the flax spinners employ the like number of foot wheels, on an open gallery, about seven feet high, erected for that purpose along one side of the room: so that the mistress has a full view of the whole number at once. This set forms two subdivisions, who work alternately three days in the week on the gallery, and the other three on the floor.

The upper room for sewing and knitting is about eighteen feet square; it is high, and well lighted on three sides. Here the youngest girls do no other work than knitting: the twenty-four eldest sew in the morning and knit in the afternoon.

Besides the mistresses attending these two rooms, a master is employed in a smaller room near the sewing-school, in instructing them as before mentioned. For this purpose, the whole number is divided into six classes of ten scholars each; and these classes are taken in rotation from the works, and remain with him, each *one hour a day*. He likewise reads an appropriate form of prayer to the whole school every morning, and keeps the account of their periods of absence and of the after-mentioned tickets. On Sundays the scholars of both schools assemble in the boys' school, where a preparatory form of prayer is used, and a psalm sung; after which they go down in procession with their master and mistresses, to the parish church, where seats are provided for them.

The apartments for the two mistresses and the master are among the buildings occupied by the female school of industry.

The salaries of these three teachers, and the expenses of fuel for all the apartments, are defrayed by the trust.

The *whole profit* of the labour of the scholars is divided among them; a small part weekly, but the bulk of it annually at Christmas, in the following manner:

The mistresses and master have tickets to distribute among them *daily* according to their diligence and good behaviour, which tickets are withdrawn, according to certain printed rules, when any faults are committed; and the annual distribution of profit is made in exact proportion to the number of tickets that each scholar has received, and preserved, during the year.

The girls all attended as day scholars until the latter end of last October, when twelve of them, between the ages of seven and nine, were admitted as inmates, and provided with food, clothing, and lodging, at the expense of the charity; towards which, however, the profits of their work are received. They chiefly consist of children living at too great a distance to attend the school, and, in the election of them, a preference was given to *orphans* and other *destitute* children. They are to remain until they are 14 or 15 years old. A cow is kept for them, which in the last year or two of their stay it is intended that they shall milk; and, as they advance in strength, they are occasionally, and in turns, to be employed in washing and mending their own clothes, in dressing their victuals, and in cleaning the rooms; by which means they will be prepared for good services, which it will be the endeavour of the trust to procure for them, with suitable encouragement for their employers and themselves.

There is every reason to hope, that the produce of the scholars' work will so much diminish the expense of their maintenance, as to enable the trustees in time to extend this benefit to a greater proportion of the whole number, without much additional charge to the charity. Every one of the twelve now admitted on this footing had learnt to spin jersey, and had knit herself one pair of stockings, and some two pairs, within the first quarter, though ignorant of both these employments before.

It only remains to state the methods taken to provide work for the children. The greatest difficulty was with regard to *sewing*. In order to bring this kind of work within their reach, handbills were distributed in the neighbouring towns and villages, giving notice, that it would be carefully performed *at one half of the usual prices;* and, by the good management of the mistress, it was so well done, that as much work as could be executed, if not more, soon came in, and still continues, from all quarters. The reduced prices are found to be as much a charity to the employers, among the labouring classes, as to the children employed. The flax is bought on the best terms; and, when spun, it is woven and bleached in the parish. By the care of the mistress and the weaver, in sorting the thread according to its quality, the cloth has proved very good and serviceable; and, after allowing the children the usual spinning prices, has abundantly repaid the cost of materials and workmanship. Wool is purchased of the farmers, after shearing-time; and a large room, with all proper conveniences, is appropriated to the use of a manufacturer, who is employed in sorting, dyeing, and combing it. The jersey, when spun, is doubled by some of the children, and then brought back to the combing-room, where there is a twisting-mill for finishing it as worsted. Part of this is sold, part employs the knitters, and a proportion is sent to two stocking-weavers at Berwick. It does not appear that there will be any difficulty, or loss, in the sale either of the stockings or of the worsted."

Schools of Industry at Kendal.

[EXTRACT.]

" THE Schools of Industry at Kendal, contain 112 children : of whom 30 of the elder girls are employed in spinning, sewing, knitting, and the work of the house; and the 36 younger girls in knitting only. Eight boys are taught *shoe-making*, and the remaining 38 are engaged in what is called *card-setting*, namely, the preparing of the machinery for carding wool; an occupation apparently difficult and intricate, but easily learnt, and peculiarly adapted to little children. For the industry-schools two mistresses are retained for knitting and spinning, at 8*s.* a week each; and a master shoemaker, whose salary (arising out of an allowance of two-pence a pair for finishing the shoes, and in fact deducted out of his scholars' earnings) amounts to 12*s.* a week. For the reading and writing school there is a master, aged 18, at half a guinea a week; and an usher, *a boy of* 14, who received, formerly, eighteen-pence a week, but, in consequence of superior offers, is now engaged at three shillings a week. These two, with the assistance of the upper and more intelligent boys, supply all the requisite instruction for these industry-schools, where 112 children are educated and fitted for useful life. The expense of the whole establishment, in salaries, fires, candles, rent, and every incidental charge (furniture, premiums, and school wages being deducted), has amounted, in two years, to only 110*l.* 1*s.* 2*d.* or 55*l.* 0*s.* 7*d.* a year. How much this small annual expenditure has effected will be detailed in the remaining pages of this extract, through which I shall direct my attention chiefly to those points in which the schools at Kendal differ from other schools. Of the boys, I have already stated that eight are employed in making shoes: this is the most expensive part of the establishment, the cost of teaching these eight boys being something more than twenty guineas a year; so that if this expense were deducted, that of teaching the other scholars would not be so much as 6*l.* 6*s.* a year, or about five farthings a week each. Perhaps, however, this art will be found to have answered better than any part of the establishment; the boys being now, at the end of 18 months, able to make shoes completely, except finishing with the knife, which is the last and most difficult part of the work: and some of them can even do this. The two best of them are not 12 years of age, and yet are capable of earning, at Kendal, from three to four shillings a week each. One of these boys would, without any apprentice-fee, be an acquisition, as an apprentice, to any master shoemaker.

The girls' schools are now, except as to their attendance on the reading-school, entirely under the direction of a committee of ladies, who regularly visit and superintend them, and who, by these means, have produced an apparent amendment in the cleanliness of their apartments and their personal appearance. The original plan for their instruction in the different kinds of kitchen work is in part executed. Breakfast is provided at the school daily, except on Saturdays and Sundays, for above 40 scholars, each of whom pays 4½*d.* a week; a sum which will barely defray the expense of provisions, without fuel. The elder girls are employed, in rotation, in assisting to prepare breakfast and in washing the utensils.

I was present at their breakfast to-day (10th of August, 1801), when abundance of very good milk porridge was served up for the children, in a cleanly and decent manner. The object attained by providing the breakfast is the punctual attendance of the children in the morning, which had been frequently prevented by the real or pretended irregularity of their breakfasts at home.

Four of the girls have been, for two or three months, learning to wash. They bring their own family linen every Friday evening, and are furnished with soap, fuel, and every necessary accommodation, *gratis.* Two have already been instructed in it, and have gone into service. Others are to be taught in their turns. The committee is preparing to erect an oven and a baking-plate, so that the girls may learn to make oaten cake and wheaten bread. It is proposed that they shall eventually be encouraged to bring oatmeal and flour from home, in order to make bread and oat cake at the schools for their respective families. This art will not only be very useful in training girls for the station of servants, but will also supply a most essential qualification for the wife of the cottager. The mode of teaching the children their letters is deserving of attention. They are taught first to copy the capital letters in sand, from a printed card; beginning with the most simple forms, as I, H, T, &c. and proceeding to those that are more complex. They then learn to copy the smaller letters in the same way, and in alphabetical order. It is very curious to observe with what readiness and correctness the youngest of these children will form letters in the sand, and how commonly they make the knowledge of them matter of amusement, and of self-gratulation.

A set of maps having been presented, and hung up in the school, Dr. Briggs adopted the idea of encouraging and stimulating the attention of the children by giving them, every week, some easy lessons in practical geography. Persons who have not visited these schools, may probably doubt (as I did) the propriety of making this a part of the education of *poor* children. Upon attending this morning, however, I have had reason to judge highly of the effects of such an addition to their instruction; and I have considered, that, should they hereafter be placed in mercantile or naval situations, such knowledge would be of essential use to them. I observed that those who gave the best answers upon this examination, were the same who carried off the prizes of industry; and I am convinced, from the information and pleasure which they displayed in this study, that spirit and energy must pervade all their other occupations."

* * * * * * * * *

EXTRACT FROM AN ACCOUNT OF

A Society for the Promotion of Industry, in the county of Essex:

By John Conyers, Esq.

"In November, 1794, a meeting was held at Epping, in Essex, to take into consideration a proposal for the promotion of Industry in that neighbourhood. An association was formed of 14 parishes, the parochial subscription being agreed to be *one per cent.* on their rates; and that of individuals not more than 5s. each. These subscriptions, with a few benefactions, produced, in 1795, the sum of 154l.; which was proposed to be set apart as a fund for the following purposes, viz.

1st. Annual presents of clothing to those children who should produce the best specimens of industry.

2d. Sums of money, not exceeding 10*l.* each, to any young person on being apprenticed or going to service, or on being married, according to the number of annual prizes such young person should have obtained.

3d. Rewards in money to poor persons who had brought up four or more children to the age of fourteen years *without parish relief ! ! !*

4th. To overseers who should have distinguished themselves in the execution of their office, and in the employment of the poor.

The Society at the same time took measures for having workrooms and teachers provided, in the different parishes, for children and destitute persons, and spinning-wheels and a supply of work for the poor at their own houses, and also for insuring to them that they should be paid by their parishes the *full price* of their work ; which, though it made a difference of only threepence or fourpence in the pound, and was a very trifling expense to the parish, became nevertheless, to the individual who received it, a very powerful reward and encouragement.

At a meeting of the Society on the 31st of December, 1795, there were 52 children who were candidates for prizes, as spinners and knitters; *and* 21 *parents, who had brought up four or more children in lawful wedlock* without parish relief ! The parents received donations, not exceeding two guineas each, varied according to the number of their children and other circumstances; and 31 of the children received presents in clothing not exceeding twenty shillings each, according to their different merits. They also received, with the premiums, certificates of good behaviour, which they consider as marks of distinction, and of which they will probably feel the benefit through life. The following is a specimen of the form of a certificate:

INDUSTRY AND GOOD BEHAVIOUR
PROCURE NOTICE AND ESTEEM.

On the 15th *day of January*, 1798, JANE SMITH *received a premium in clothing, of the value of twenty shillings, from the* SOCIETY *of* INDUSTRY, *for the hundreds of Ongar and Harlow, and the half-hundred of Waltham, in the county of Essex, for her good behaviour, and for her skill and industry in spinning worsted.*

JOHN CONYERS, Chairman.

In the ensuing year an equal number of parents received donations on account of the families they had brought up; and clothing, to the amount of 36*l.* 15*s.*, was given to 37 children who had then produced the required specimens of industry in spinning, knitting, and plain needlework. In the present year (Jan. 1798) donations of clothing have been made to 61 industrious children, to the amount of 51*l.* 13*s.*; and the sum of 23*l.* 12*s.* 6*d.* has been given on account of the families which they have brought up.

N.B. The five foregoing articles on "SCHOOLS of INDUSTRY" are extracted from the first, second, and third volumes of the Reports of the " *Society for bettering the Condition of the Poor,*" a work to which all persons engaged in similar pursuits of benevolence would do well to refer. These Reports contain practical instructions on a great variety of subjects relating to the welfare of the POOR; and many of them are peculiarly adapted to the present times of *increasing* public distress.

School of Industry at Ipswich:

By a benevolent Individual.

THIS Lady, in a letter to a friend, expresses her conviction that *active employment*, during the largest portion of their time, is of the first importance to persons in the lower stations of life. And she considers that *one hour in a week*, strict attention being paid, is sufficient for the instruction of the girls under her superintendance in spelling, reading, and writing.

The school opens daily with reading the Scriptures, in which the children are well instructed. After which the morning is occupied in plain useful needlework; and the afternoon in platting of straw, which is found to answer very well. The latter is not recommended as a permanent employment for young women, but rather as one by which a livelihood may be obtained during ill health, or when out of service. It has been found of particular advantage in this school that it is divided into 8 classes, directed by 16 monitors for each employment; half of whom form the upper class, and the other half are engaged in instructing their companions. As they are changed weekly, these monitors have opportunities of receiving instruction in their turn, and this varying of the school offices imparts a degree of alertness to their exertions. The monitors are chosen according to their superiority in the different occupations, viz. the best readers for reading, the best sempstresses for needlework, and so on. It is observed that the mistress who superintends the straw-plat department should understand it well, otherwise it will not succeed.

Schools at Dorking.

THE neighbourhood of Dorking is remarkable for the benevolence of the gentry whose beautiful villas are scattered around, and
who kindly endeavour to render the condition of the poor comfortable; not by charitable donations merely, but by stimulating them to
industry, and by inculcating principles which tend to make them,
eventually, independent of eleemosynary assistance.

There are several well-regulated schools for the poor in and near
this town, the greater number of which are under the direction
of the more affluent inhabitants, who take pleasure in visiting
them. Reading, writing, and ciphering are taught on the respective systems of Bell and Lancaster; a strict regard is paid to the
moral and religious instruction of the children; and they are exercised in various kinds of useful *employment*. The girls practise
every sort of plain needlework, and are permitted to make up
new garments for themselves and their families, and to repair
their old ones.

The boys, besides the usual school instruction for the poor, are
taught to *knit stockings*. In the COLD HARBOUR School this employment is resorted to after the lessons are finished. When the
first pair is completed, it is given to the knitter, as an encouragement; and one pair on every ten is given for the succeeding ones.

In the school in HEMPSTEAD LANE, 24 girls are instructed
on the Lancasterian plan, by the liberality of a single family subscription. They are all clothed annually, and are retained in the
school until situations, as *house-servants*, are provided for them.

The following are the Rules observed in this School, which was
established in 1805:

1st. The children to come in the morning, punctually at 9 o'clock,
and stay till 12. In the afternoon, to come at 2 o'clock and stay
till 5; or, in the winter, till 4 o'clock.

2d. To come with their faces, heads, and hands clean, and their
clothes perfectly neat.

3d. To work from 9 till 11 in the morning; to write and cipher,
on alternate days, till 12; to spell and read from 2 till 3; to work
the rest of the afternoon.

4th. The schoolmistress to read a psalm, or other portion of
Scripture, when the school duties are ended, both morning and
afternoon. The children to be questioned afterwards on what
they have heard.

5th. To work, every Tuesday, for their own families, if they
can bring what is either clean or new.

6th. To have a half-holiday on the Saturday afternoon, and not on any other, without leave from the mistress, to whom they must give a good reason for asking one.

7th. To have a month's holiday in *gleaning-time*, and a week's holiday at Christmas.

8th. The mistress to make a cross in the book of offences, when any girl commits a fault mentioned therein:* the girl is likewise to wear a card of disgrace. This book is always to lie on the table.

9th. If there are but few crosses in the book, the children to be rewarded at the end of each quarter. Whatever money they receive at the school, to be placed in separate bags, and distributed to the respective owners at Christmas, for the purpose of purchasing clothing. Every child who has no cross marked in the offence-book during the quarter, to receive 6*d*. in addition to the usual rewards. One cross for *lying* or *stealing* to deprive the child of every reward for the quarter.

10th. The mistress to hear the children their Catechism every Wednesday afternoon.

11th. The children to attend the Sunday-Schools, and their respective places of worship, regularly.

12th. The mistress to read these rules every Monday morning.

N.B. It is calculated that about 500 children receive instruction in the several schools at Dorking. In some of these schools the parents are required to pay 3*d*. per week for each child, upon the principle that more value is commonly attached by the poor to that for which they pay *something*, than to that for which they pay *nothing*.

We have already observed that a spirit of philanthropy prevails among the more affluent inhabitants of this neighbourhood; and we are gratified in learning that several gentlemen have lately cultivated FLAX on their estates, for the express purpose of employing the poor; and that a newly invented machine for working this valuable staple, without the process of *dew-rotting*, has been introduced; though the plan is not yet brought to perfection.

We intend noticing the "*Dorking Provident Institution*" in a subsequent part of this work; and we believe it will be found to be the most complete model yet produced, of institutions of this nature.

Independently of the latter, a *Saving Bank* has been established in this town, which succeeds well.

---

* The Book of Offences has a number of columns ruled in it, under the following titles: | Month. | Date. | Absent. | Quarrelling. | Irregularity. | Dirt. | Lying. | Disobedience. | Theft. | Idleness. | Talking.

OBSERVATIONS ON

Schools of Industry.

HAVING now presented the reader with various plans, by which the children of the poor have, in different parts of this country, been successfully instructed in early habits of industry, and some of which plans, we would hope, may be found suitable in almost every neighbourhood, we cannot forbear expressing our earnest solicitude, that a subject of such vital importance to the welfare of the poor, may receive that consideration from the public, to which it is entitled.

Notwithstanding that schools for educating the children of the poor, on the systems of BELL or LANCASTER, are instituted in almost every city and to wn, and even in many villages, throughout England, it is a lamentable truth, which is proved by the crowded state of our prisons, that juvenile *offences* have increased in an alarming degree beyond all former precedent. How then is this paradox to be explained, except we suppose that some radical defect must exist in these systems? That defect, we believe, will be found to consist in the *want* of manual *employment* which, we contend, children ought to be initiated into at a very tender age: it matters not in what particular manner, so long as the *habit* of industry be formed early; and the importance of this principle, must be our apology for so often repeating the sentiment in these pages.

Education, as it respects the poor, may yet be considered as in a state of infancy in this country. The extraordinary degree of interest lately excited and felt is, however, likely to lead to very important results. The adoption of so great a variety of plans and regulations, as we every where meet with in the different charitable institutions dispersed through England, must lead us gradually nearer to some point of preference concerning these plans. While the question of the propriety of instructing the lower classes in reading and writing remains unattended by *facts*, we have no certain grounds on which to form a general decision concerning it. Consequently, these classes will, for the present, most generally, continue to be so instructed. The topic of a constant and unceasing use of the needle amongst females, so strenuously urged by our forefathers, had its origin in a strong conviction of the necessity of habits of industry, and of the intimate connection between a moral course of conduct and a perpetual application of the bodily faculties to some useful end. Could we believe otherwise, we should view the decision as a tyrannical and oppressive one. The same reflection occurs with respect to the occupations of the juvenile poor: certainly nothing should be forced upon their faculties or attention further than as it promises to be ultimately profitable to themselves and beneficial to society. To this point of most desirable information and certainty it is to be hoped we are now hastening. And the writer of this work expresses his most ardent desire that, amidst the variety of our own institutions, our national pride will not overlook what must be allowed to be an improved system, even in a foreign one. The reader is therefore presented with the following account of

A NEW AND REMARKABLE PLAN OF

Education in Switzerland.

IN this Institution *employment* and order are so blended with moral and religious instruction, as to have produced the most extraordinary results among boys formerly of vicious habits, and profligate characters. By a judicious system of training, these boys have become as remarkable for good conduct, industry, and every moral virtue, as they were before notorious for vice and irregularity.

To enable the reader to form a correct idea of this extraordinary system of education, we shall give a brief outline of the plan ; chiefly drawn from a small pamphlet, entitled " *Reports of the School of Industry at Hofwyl, in the Canton of Berne in Switzerland;*" translated from the Bibliotheque Britannique, published at Geneva in 1814.

Previously to the Revolution in France, the Swiss were deservedly considered an industrious, frugal, and virtuous people. Like the Scotch, they appear to have appreciated the advantages of education, and to have been aware that by its means not only their moral condition would be improved, but their comforts and happiness augmented.

About the year 1810, a remarkable Institution for the Education of Poor Boys was founded at HOFWYL, in the canton of Berne, under the sole direction and at the entire charge of M. FELLENBERG, a gentleman in whose character the greatest benevolence was united with an extensive knowledge of human nature. In this undertaking he was assisted by THOMAS VEHRLI, a schoolmaster of Turgovia, a young man who possessed a kind heart, as well as a most persevering zeal, even to a degree of enthusiasm which enabled him to surmount the greatest difficulties.

A trial of their benevolent scheme was made on a farm of about 200 acres of land. The school opened with 23 boys, mostly of the poorest description; but it has since increased to the number of about 30. The children of the idle, the destitute, and the beggar, were indiscriminately admitted into this asylum, and became the objects of its care equally with those of honest or industrious parents. They generally entered it in a miserable plight, many of them with vicious habits, and some with dispositions to rebel; but these were subdued by a firm but mild discipline, and the most perverse tempers yielded to gentle treatment, affection, and order.

The kind and generous Vehrli began by partaking of their plain food, which consisted of potatoes and milk; and slept with them on their beds of straw. He submitted cheerfully to these privations; and, by thus associating with the children, wrought most powerfully on their affections. A trial of some months proved that Vehrli's qualifications were admirably adapted to his station; whilst it discovered the purity of his mind, his uprightness, and zeal. He was fully aware of the important trust he was about to take upon himself, and of the necessity of setting a good example to the children under his care. Always diligent in his occupations, he was sensible of the great advantages that his country would derive from a rational and useful mode of educating the poor; such as would tend to secure to the indigent but industrious labourer a happy existence, and to banish from him idleness, vice, and misery, the certain causes of poverty.

In short, this extraordinary young man believed himself specially called to take part in this Institution; in which he proved how much good a devoted mind, joined with an upright intention, is capable of effecting, in the execution of a most arduous design: nor was his zeal herein to be restrained.

While Vehrli was thus destined to act a conspicuous part in this noble charity, as a schoolmaster, the experienced and intelligent mind of Fellenberg, the benevolent founder, was actively engaged in perfecting the plan and in superintending the execution of it. And having now brought it to a degree of satisfactory excellence, he designs it as a legacy to his adopted children, his pupils, whom he has qualified to fill the stations of directors of agricultural institutions, or of agricultural servants.

EMPLOYMENT.—When the weather permits, the boys work in the fields: they pick up stones, weed, or transplant, clean the walks, glean corn, and are variously occupied on the farm, in driving or guiding the horses at the plough, carrying out manure, and in other business of husbandry suitable to their age and strength. They have a little cart drawn by an ass, which is almost always in motion; and in many respects these boys perform the work of men.

If the weather does not permit them to work in the fields, they employ themselves in weaving baskets, and in platting straw for chairs or mats: they make fagots, saw and split wood, cut up roots for the fire, and thresh corn: they also pick and sort wool, and prepare flax, within-doors. Some of the elder boys work as carpenters and wheelwrights, and make and repair tools and implements of husbandry. They sometimes mix and apply colours in painting. In long evenings and in wet weather the boys learn to knit and mend their stockings, and to make and mend their shoes.

About ten hours in each day are devoted to the several sorts of manual labour. But though labour is considered the main object of the Institution, mental instruction is not neglected; for, as Vehrli generally works with his pupils, he proposes questions in arithmetic, and otherwise exercises their mental faculties, whilst they are thus engaged. Work, however, is not allowed to be retarded even by instructive questions; the boy who ceases to work, in order to attend to conversation (whether he be gleaning corn or performing other business in the field), is sent down to the bottom of the rank.

M. Fellenberg, every morning, appoints the labours of the day, and Vehrli gives the orders to the boys; and as it cannot be supposed that they all attend to the same employment, he contrives to be with the most numerous party. A journal of the work, and the names of those by whom it is performed, is entered by Vehrli every evening, or, with his assistance, by one of the senior boys.

In every part of their employment the attention of the boys is kept alive; their bodily powers become strong by exercise, whilst their intellectual faculties are at the same time cultivated and developed. The means devised appear well calculated to produce intelligent and industrious labourers, who will prove a treasure to their country.

With regard to *manner*, every thing is done with neatness and exactness: it is considered a loss of time to do business in a slovenly or careless manner.

DISTRIBUTION OF TIME.—In summer the boys rise at five o'clock, and in winter at six. After they have dressed themselves and said their prayers, they receive instruction for an hour. They then breakfast, and afterwards work until half-past eleven, when they have half an hour for dinner. Vehrli then gives them a lesson during one hour. They then work out of doors until six o'clock. When their supper is finished, they receive further instruction, which concludes with prayer; and they are generally in bed between 8 and 9 o'clock.

This distribution of time varies, nevertheless, according to the seasons. In winter the instruction is given before supper, during from one to two hours. For the most part of the year the *sedentary* instruction lasts for *three* hours only; in winter, however, it occupies *five* or *six* hours of the day. Page 2.

INSTRUCTION.—The subjects of instruction are reading, writing, drawing, singing, and calculation or arithmetic: the boys generally write on slates, excepting on Saturdays, when the elder ones write with a pen. They acquire some knowledge of grammar and geometry; and the daily phenomena and productions of nature are occasionally explained to them. They learn the geography and history of their country, too, as far as these may be useful to them. They are also engaged in mental exercises, and receive *religious* and *moral* instruction, of which we shall speak hereafter. No regular order is observed in the distribution of their lessons; the attention of the children is directed to one subject or another, according as circumstances direct.

The teacher observes that experience justifies this method, and that it has no inconvenience in cases in which *instruction is only a recreation from work*: but he admits that when instruction* is the main object, the minds of pupils should be *steadily* exercised to the acquirement of it.

DRAWING in this school is very simple: the exercises are performed chiefly upon large slates, with common chalk.

" Drawing," says the Reporter, " may be considered as the basis of the art of writing. It serves to make us acquainted with sensible objects, of which *language* only gives an imperfect description. It is one of the most ancient, as well as the most natural modes of writing. In this point of view, and as connected with all the useful arts, *drawing* should form an essential part of poor children's instruction, as well as of that of the higher classes of Society."

Amongst the greatest obligations received from Pestalozzi, relative to the education of the poor, is the method which he introduced into elementary schools. The mass of the people consist of mechanics; and in order to *describe* their tools, it is necessary that the construction and arrangement of the several parts of them should be understood. It is difficult to succeed in any trade without the aid of the pencil. It is required in estimating the contents and size of vessels, and of all solid bodies. Drawing, in short, forms and exercises the *eye*, and thus leads to that clearness of judgment which is necessary for success in most of the daily operations of rural life.—Pages 4, 5.

---

* The meaning of the word instruction here seems to be unduly limited. Instruction is commonly *practical* in its effects, though always *preceptive* in its form. The processes of ploughing and reaping, and of every kind of manual labour, are taught *preceptively* in the first instance, as truly as reading, writing, &c. It is probable, therefore, that the teacher only means to make a distinction between *mental exercise* and *manual labour;* and intimates that, whichever happens to be the main object in education, the other may be resorted to as an amusement.—ED.

ARITHMETIC begins by Pestalozzi's calculations, and proceeds by practical applications of them. The result hitherto is, that more than half the pupils are masters of the first four rules, are acquainted with the rule of three, and are able to work any rule with fractions. It was proposed to them to divide into two, four, and eight equal parts, a space of land 49,000 feet in length, and 27,000 in breadth: they not only answered to those questions with promptitude, but gave an account of the manner of their calculations, and of the foundation on which they rested.—Page 6.

GRAMMAR.—Though a complete course of grammatical instruction cannot be entered into in a school of this description, the scholars receive sufficient instruction concerning it for the common purposes of language: they know the difference between substantives and adjectives, and between verbs and adverbs. One of the exercises of the second class (whilst Vehrli is employed with the first) is, to join with any given substantive as many adjectives as they can find, and to write them on their slates. This method, which is adopted when the boys read, enables them to express themselves more correctly than children educated in other schools, and without the least hesitation. Most of them express themselves with grammatical propriety in writing as well as in speaking.—P. 9.

GEOMETRY.—The Reporter remarks, with respect to Geometry, that if it appear to be out of its place in a *village school*, yet, as a practical science, it must be acknowledged to be useful to persons of the lower classes. In order to observe surrounding objects with precision, we should know what a right, a bent or curved, or a parallel line is; as also what are right, obtuse, and acute angles, circles, triangles, cubes, cylinders, and spheres: and although there are, in the class of men who are deemed well-instructed, a thousand individuals ignorant of such matters, it is certain that, without some knowledge of them, they can never form correct notions of the objects that daily fall under their observation. It is very desirable that a husbandman should know how to measure the height and contents of a tree, or the extent of a field; and, in this view, a little geometry is necessary to the lowest peasant. For this reason it is that geometry constitutes a part of the instruction given to the POOR at HOFWYL.—Page 10.

NATURAL HISTORY.—The principal design in teaching natural history is to give children some knowledge of the nature of the objects they daily meet with. At Hofwyl they are taught to know not only all the useful plants in agriculture, but every plant that grows in the country, and even those which we call weeds. They can distinguish the stones that are found in the fields, according to their names and different qualities. One of the children attempted, in our presence, a sketch of natural history, as far as he knew it: this was a boy who, not long before, had, with his parents, obtained a livelihood by *begging on the highways!* He was taken up and put into a house of correction, and from thence he was almost immediately removed to the Institution at Hofwyl. —Page 11.

READING.—Almost all the children on their arrival knew their letters, but scarcely one could read well; at present most of them know how to read with a facility, a clearness, and an expression, of which there are but few examples to be found in schools of this kind.—Page 4.

During the evening one of the elder pupils reads aloud to the others some interesting book : the master ascertains whether they have been attentive or not, by questioning them on what has been read.   He gives them an opportunity of forming a judgment, in a moral point of view, of the events and personages described ; and it happens, most frequently, that their observations are un-usually just.—Page 12.

NOTES OF THE BOYS.—The journal which the pupils keep is a very good exercise.   On Saturday morning they write down on their slates whatever has appeared to them deserving of notice during the preceding week; and, when Vehrli has corrected the performances, they write them in books.   These books (which are voluminous) contain an account of the week's work, whether in the fields or in the house; the trifling events of the school; ob-servations on vegetation; remarkable events noticed in reading; or whatever they have learned in the week that is new.   Some-times, instead of remarks, may be found a hymn or a drawing. The inspectors have found, in these journals, a fund of good sense and acute observations; they remark that they are written without the least blot or mistake, which is rarely to be found in the written exercises of poor children.—*Ibid.*

INSTRUCTION COMBINED WITH WORK.—It is observed that Vehrli does not *confine* himself to *three hours of instruction* in the day ; since, during their work in the fields, at table, and at play, he never fails to teach them something.   In a letter to a friend he writes thus, "I instruct them at all hours of the day, without disturbing them at their work; I engage them as much as possible in instructive conversation.   I find that the open fields and the ' book of nature' afford means of calling forth the obser-vation, and exercising the reflection of children, not to be found in the dull routine of a school-room; where, shut up within four dark walls, their time is not unfrequently wasted in indolence or languor: mine, on the contrary, become every day more intelli-gent and active.

"I have made some remarks on the following problem, which I have often proposed to myself: *Can* INSTRUCTION *be com-bined with* WORK ?   And in what manner can instruction be the most easily given to children without interfering with their work? Instruction can be united with some, but not with all kinds of work. As the mind of man is never at rest, the minds of children must share the common activity; and they should have something to employ them in a *useful* way. It is for this end that I endeavour to discover, during our conversations of the evening, what are their ideas; which of them has, during the day, learned the most, observed the most, and retained the best. I have found this method very useful, because it renders observation pleasureable to them. I often hear one boy say to another, 'Ah, ah, I know a very curious thing, and I will tell it this evening to Vehrli.' I also give them, very often in a morning, a problem to solve. For example; I say to one, find for me, during the day, twenty substantives beginning with an A, which are things belonging to a well-furnished house. I say to another, find for me twenty-five substantives, which are things that can only be seen when we look at the sky. From a third I require, in the day, thirty adjectives, which can be joined to the word *house*. When they have time, they write upon a slate the words they have found.—Page 14.

"Concerning GEOGRAPHY, these are the trifling problems I give them: name me twelve towns in Switzerland, the initial letters of which follow in alphabetical order; and tell me in what Cantons they are situated. I give the same problem for rivers, expecting the pupils to tell me their sources, and every particular relating to the mountains, vallies, and lakes: for this purpose it is necessary to have a map, at which the children may look whenever they please. By following this method the progress of the boys is very rapid, without making the least sacrifice of their manual occupations. In this manner their minds are employed when they are at work in the fields; and, during the hours of recreation, they look for the places on the map, or else request their master to point them out for them."—Page 15.

The following exercise appears particularly useful: one of the children is asked to find four things above six feet in length, and to shew them in the evening; or else to give a list of twelve things, four of them being five feet in height; four, six feet in breadth; and four, eight feet in length. These exercises are doubly instructive; they form the eye for observation, and develop the faculty of attention. Such exercises not having been used in schools, the reason becomes obvious why children so soon forget what they learn; it is for want of a *practical application* of it. The following exercise appears not less useful: "My children, you must each give me five problems of arithmetic to resolve: let me see which of you will give me the most curious ones, and which will be the best judge of the manner in which I resolve them.

"It is very interesting to see how the children endeavour to find out the most puzzling problems for me. When we are at work in the fields, likewise, I frequently employ them in spelling words.

" Every thing we undertake is a means of developing their natural, and heretofore dormant faculties. We lose no opportunity of instructing them; and there is scarcely any daily occurrence from which the boys cannot learn something, *provided they are not treated like creatures without understanding*, but are made attentive to useful points, and obliged to explain the reason and the use of every thing."—Page 16.

RELIGIOUS INSTRUCTION.—Of this kind, *singing* is considered to form a part. Vehrli observes, " Singing is always to me the most agreeable and the most cheerful occupation. The moment at which I feel most pleased is when I am engaged in singing with some of ' my children.' It is a means of awakening religious emotions; and upon this account a good selection of hymns would be a very useful acquisition. Fine musical compositions elevate and delight the mind: I find that they inspire good thoughts which would never have found access otherwise. The Apostle Paul must have well known the effect singing has on our hearts, when he invites us, in his Epistle to the Ephesians, to ' sing psalms and hymns together for our edification.' [Here several instances are given in which singing godly songs and hymns have proved both instructive and edifying to the children.] Vehrli observes, ' a favourite hymn with the children begins thus ; ' The time GOD grants us flies with rapidity ;' and we always sing it at the conclusion of our discourse on a Saturday evening. How often has it happened that the spectators have been affected at our performance! Indeed, to listen to these children singing a hymn from Lavater or Mildheim, with such expression, and to consider at the same time what they are, compared with what they were, makes it impossible not to be moved even to tears."—Page 8.

DEVOTION.—Every Sunday the boys have service in Mr. Fellenberg's hall, and all the pupils of the Institution attend there. It is the only place of meeting with the pupils of the upper school, which adds much to the solemnity of this act of devotion. On the whole, it would be difficult to imagine an education more truly religious than these children have, though they are not at first taught a complete system of doctrine: all the purest ideas of *Deity* and *Providence*, suitable to their age, are selected for their instruction. The popular works put into their hands contain a truly practical morality; but the instructions which Vehrli occasionally imparts have a more certain effect, inasmuch as they apply immediately to the particulars of their life. In this respect, also, let the journal of the master inform us. He observes, " Children may at an early age be instructed in the knowledge of GOD, without the assistance of religious books. One fine evening, we went out all together into the fields: the sky was clear, a faint twilight was still perceptible in the west; on the other side, the moon arose majestically above the mountains, it was at the full, and peculiarly beautiful; it shone with extraordinary lustre on the sheet of water which lay before us: my children gazed with rapture on the expanse of the firmament, but the moon particularly attracted their attention; when two of them began to sing the hymn, the first words of which are, 'The orb of night which rises in silence:' we all joined. I took this opportunity of reminding them that GOD had created all those beautiful objects which they then contemplated; and when we returned home, I read to them the hymn which begins thus, 'There is a GOD who watches over us;' which had a great effect upon their youthful hearts: they conversed together on this beautiful evening until sleep overcame them.

"Delighted so soon to behold the fruit of my labours, I resolved thus to seize every opportunity of instructing them concerning the omnipresence, the majesty, the wisdom, and goodness of GOD. Last autumn we were overtaken in the fields by a violent thunder storm. We hastened home; when I called the boys together, and read a hymn to them on this subject: I made them sensible that GOD never ceases to be merciful to us; I explained to them the use of storms, and made them comprehend what thunder and lightning were. I told them that those only who had committed bad actions should be affrighted, but that the good should be thankful to GOD for all that he does for his creatures. I sometimes take occasion from the fruitful rain and the refreshing dew to remind them that GOD is the best and most bountiful of fathers towards the children of men."—Page 30.

"In our morning conversation, I endeavour to render habitual to their minds a sense of gratitude towards that GOD who blesses us with calm repose, and gives us strength to fulfil our daily labours. In the evening I recall their reflections and emotions to the same objects. During our meals I am careful to remind them that they are indebted to GOD for the capability of enjoying food: I explain to them that man may labour to provide food, but the health and skill that render labour useful proceed from GOD alone; and that the only way in which we can testify our gratitude is to employ, in a proper manner, the strength that each repast imparts. In thus acting, I conceive I use more efficacious means than if I made them at first repeat forms of prayer. Experience shows that customary prayers before or after meals have little or no effect; they are the mere semblance of devotion. How much better to excite gratitude by shewing the great use we derive from water and fire, plants and animals; and teaching them that GOD has created all these for the use of man! Religious thoughts and religious affections are the best guides for the direction of life. I ask, what is man without *religion*? These, then, are the first thoughts and first feelings that should be inculcated."—Page 31.

RELIGION continued.—" When during our labours in the field various phenomena appear and circumstances occur, as they often do, which give rise to some interesting question, I seize the opportunity to instruct the boys in the existence of GOD and his attributes, in a manner that makes a deep impression. I inform them that we are blessed with the knowledge of GOD, and of his conduct towards man, in the Holy Scriptures, wherein he has revealed his designs with respect to us; and that such is his goodness to man, that he has sent his only Son into the world to teach us his will and to lead us into all good.

" When I see my children in a proper frame of mind, I read to them, out of the New Testament, extracts from the life and doctrine of Jesus, and I teach them that he is the most perfect model that we can choose for imitation."—Page 32.

To the foregoing account of the religious exercises of this school, it may be added, that the business of each day begins with *prayer,* and ends with the same. Singing hymns or psalms appears also to be regularly used by the boys, as an act of devotion. Vehrli observes, " singing, instead of being a vain sound, without any heartfelt emotion, is, with them, the exercise of animated feelings, and thereby becomes real prayer."—Page 28.

RECREATION.—Although the business of this Inttitution is so happily diversified, that the ordinary occupations of the boys are in themselves a recreation, they have, besides, some few diversions, which tend to invigorate their constitutions. These are of an athletic kind, such as running, leaping, jumping, balancing, climbing trees, bathing and swimming in the summer season ; and, in winter, skating on the ice.

CLEANLINESS.—This is especially attended to, which is the more necessary as work in the fields is frequently dirty. Every morning the children wash their hands and face; again they wash their hands at noon, and in the evening before they sit down to table ; and when they have worked barefoot, they wash their feet before they go to bed.—Page 27.

CLOTHING.—The children's clothing is, in summer, of coarse cotton; in winter, of woollen cloth : they go with their feet bare, except occasionally, when their work in the fields obliges them to wear shoes and stockings. They always go without any thing on their heads. Most of them know how to mend their own clothes.—Page 2.

FOOD.—The children are fed like country servants: their breakfast consists of soup, composed chiefly of vegetables, or bread and milk ; their dinner and supper are of the same, with the addition of potatoes : on Sunday the children get meat for dinner. Their bread varies according to the price of the corn of which it is made; it is a mixture of wheat and rye, barley, or beans, in different proportions. Vehrli, seated at the top of the table, presides at all their meals, and helps the children. In the longest days of summer, when the supper is late, the children get bread and fruit between dinner and supper. The inspectors have ever been satisfied that the food was perfectly wholesome and good, and that there was always the greatest abundance at their table.—Page 3.

PUNISHMENTS.—The punishments are few, but efficacious, short, and serious: they consist chiefly of remonstrances, sometimes made privately, and sometimes in the presence of other children, according to the exigency. The offender is sometimes excluded from the public repast. Frequently, when they commit a fault, they condemn *themselves*, and absent themselves from table. Vehrli, on these occasions, sends them their portion to their room, *somewhat diminished*. Corporal punishments are seldom necessary for the younger ones, and only at their first coming to Hofwyl: a cane is the instrument applied in such cases. "As to the elder ones," observes Vehrli, "if a parental remonstrance is not sufficient, I use, in preference to blows, a sharp remonstrance in private, or a mortification in presence of their companions. When I am obliged to have recourse to corporal punishment, I seldom inflict it immediately after the offence. I suspend it, to give the child time for reflection. After remonstrating with the offender, and making him sensible that punishment is intended for his good, I give him one or two strokes with the cane on each hand. When punishments are thus inflicted, the effect is certain; but he who chastises in a passion, without giving time for reflection, is very blameable, and acts in opposition to the whole design of education."—Page 35.

REWARDS.—No rewards are bestowed but the satisfaction and approbation of the master. All distinctions, which tend to flatter the vanity of the boys, or excite their envy, are banished from the institution. Vehrli observes, in his journal, "Some of them are extremely alive to any commendation which may be given in the evening conversation to the deserving, or to any reproof to the undeserving. In that peaceful hour of recollection, when all my children are united in heart, what a delight it is to them to hear me declare that *I am satisfied with them, and that they have done their duty!* They are equally afflicted when I reproach them with some neglect; he who finds himself in the latter situation, is painfully sensible that he is the only one who must retire to rest without my shaking his hand and wishing him 'good night.' But it is not right to appear, next morning, as if nothing had happened, and caress the child as usual; we must persevere for two or three days, or longer, till an amendment has taken place. It is thus that an amendment is effected. To appear in the same moment pleased and displeased, is only creating *indifference* to every command."—Page 36.

REFLECTIONS.—Having now given an epitome of the plan adopted in this admirable Institution, though the extracts we have made already exceed the limits we had assigned them, we cannot take leave of a subject so interesting without making a few summary observations.

When we reflect that a number of poor children, whose connexions were of the lowest description, and whose habits were vicious and idle, have been so changed by the treatment we have been describing, as to become (if we may adopt the expression) " new creatures;" that they have acquired habits of order, industry, and virtue, and are thus qualified to fill respectable and useful stations in society; the astonishing effect produced by this judicious management excites our sincerest admiration. Withdrawn from bad examples, and protected from temptations to vice, and having constantly before them examples of every thing good and virtuous, these children feel no inducement to rebel or to return to their former bad habits. They resemble a well-regulated community, every member of which fills his proper station of usefulness, and where every thing is conducted with beautiful harmony, founded upon principles of regularity and order. Of such a system of education, we are ready to exclaim, Happy indeed and enviable the lot of every child placed under the fostering kindness and care of the Institution at Hofwyl!

PECUNIARY ESTIMATES OF THIS INSTITUTION.

The expense incurred in this Institution was, in the early part of it, calculated at about 9*l.* per head per annum; and the return for the labour of the boys, averaged at nearly half their cost. The total expenditure for the three first years, from 1810 to 1813, after deducting the produce of the children's labour, amounted to 83 livres, 16 sols. and 6 den. or equal to 6*l.* yearly for each pupil. —Page 63.

It is further stated, in page 65, that " Mr. Fellenberg hopes to prove, ultimately, that such institutions can support themselves." Whether his subsequent experience has confirmed this hope, we have not learnt. But were the expense, in England, larger for each boy than is here stated, we believe it would be less than what is usually paid in most parts of England for maintaining the children of the poor in a *parish workhouse,* where little more is learnt than idleness and vice.

Under a system like the one before us, from which the moral and physical advantages, both to the children and to the community, are so incalculably great, the pecuniary expenses, were they even larger, ought not to prevent us from making the experiment. We do not say that the *plan* can be strictly followed in all cases, but we presume the *principle* may, without exception.

In short, give to the children of the poor, an education like that at Hofwyl, and you will secure to the labouring classes that degree of manly independence to which they are entitled by nature, and which will enable them in time to assist others, *as well as to take care of themselves.*

☞ Having thus described several judicious and instructive plans for initiating the *juvenile* poor into early habits of industry and virtue, we proceed to offer some practical suggestions for the employment of the *adult* poor; a subject of peculiar importance in the present calamitous state of the country.

A SUMMARY ACCOUNT OF

An Association in Dublin, for the Suppression of Mendicity;

(Chiefly drawn from the Second Report, to the year ending 1819.)

MENDICITY, the offspring of idleness or improvidence, is most usually accompanied with profligacy and vice. Assuming the appearance of real distress, it imposes upon the feelings of the humane and charitable, who, while they are yielding to an impulse of nature in relieving the distressed, do not perceive that they are betrayed into an error that occasions great disorder in society.

It is observable that mendicity prevails most where the greatest provision is made for the poor, by means of public or private charities. Charity is one of the first of Christian virtues, when rightly directed; but it degenerates into weakness, and gives encouragement to idleness and vice, when mistaken or misguided in its application. There is only one safe and unerring principle, by which the poor can be permanently and effectually relieved, namely, by enabling them to become *the instruments of helping themselves.* All other means are but temporary or fallacious; especially if we attempt to contravene the first great law of our omniscient Creator, who decreed that the wants of his creatures should be supplied by labour.

In England there appears to be little or no excuse for the disgraceful practice of street-begging; where the enormous sum of nine millions yearly is now drawn from the public, for the maintenance of the poor; besides what private charities produce. In this country all who are really in distress may obtain relief from their proper parishes.

In Ireland, where the same legal provision for the distressed poor is not made, they are, for the most part, relieved either by the private benevolence of individuals or by means of public contributions raised for that particular purpose.

We may observe that during the last thirty years mendicity has been increasing in Ireland nearly in the same proportion in which pauperism, its sister evil, has been spreading itself in so alarming a manner in England; and, probably, the causes in which it originated are similar to those of pauperism.

Whether we trace these evils to the desolating influence of a long and expensive war, to the consequent increase of taxation, to a scarcity of employment among the labouring classes, or to the insufficiency of the wages they receive, compared with the high price of the necessaries of life, there can be no doubt of their actual existence.

The great and alarming increase of poverty and mendicity among the lower classes, in the Irish capital, appears, about three years since, to have excited the serious apprehension of a number of gentlemen in that city, who were distinguished as well by their high stations in society as their eminent talents for business. These gentlemen having formed themselves into an Association, endeavoured to lay down a plan for arresting the progress of a nuisance which had arrived at a height, not only exceedingly troublesome and disgraceful, but dangerous to the peace and good order of society. They found that the obstacles they had to contend with were numerous and extensive, and that nothing short of an unreserved appropriation of their time and talents would prove sufficient to overcome them. But though the difficulties were formidable, and the obstacles discouraging, an ardent and persevering zeal, joined to a high sense of public duty, enabled them finally to triumph over all opposition.

In their endeavours to remove, or even to lessen an evil so deeply seated in the depravity of human nature, it was necessary that the Committee should act like skilful physicians, namely, that they should first ascertain the cause of the disorder, and then apply a remedy best adapted to its cure. Considering therefore that as Infinite Wisdom had ordained *labour* to be the instrument of correcting our first parent, after he had transgressed the divine law, they wisely concluded that no means would prove so salutary and effectual, towards reforming the idle and vicious, as employment. The propriety of this determination has since been confirmed by the surprizing moral advantages that have resulted from the employment of the female criminals in the British Metropolis in Newgate, under the direction of a *female Howard*. The system adopted there is one in which moral and religious instruction is judiciously combined with useful employment. In all situations and circumstances, labour, or the constant and useful occupation of time, will be found to afford the most effectual means, not only of restoring the idle and vicious to order and virtue, but for the prevention of crime.

It was on these principles that the "Society for the Suppression of Mendicity in Dublin" commenced their operations. By their 2d Report it will appear that "the first species of labour which they introduced among the mendicants, was that of *sweeping the streets;* but this was adopted rather as an experiment, the adoption of which soon convinced them that the nature of the employment was not well calculated to accomplish the objects they had in view." They observe, " that they have ever held in mind that the suppression of a nuisance does not constitute their *sole* aim: with them rests a duty of a more important nature,—to *reform,* if possible, the *evil* habits which are the certain result of that nuisance." They have found that, without more rigid superintendance than the state of their funds allowed of, "not only would the broom be thrown aside, but the old trade of *begging* be occasionally resorted to. Besides, a life spent in the public streets, however active, is not calculated to effect any *moral change;* nor is it suited to females, to which sex the necessitous poor, in this city, chiefly belong."

The next kind of employment for the male poor, which the Committee made trial of, was that of pulverising oyster-shells for manure : they were informed that it had answered in the parish of St. Martin's, London, where a considerable number of poor persons had been beneficially employed in this way. "The simplicity of the process at once struck them, and the facility of procuring the materials necessary to make the experiment induced them to give it an immediate trial ; the result of which proved that this employment combines precisely the objects required ; with the additional advantages of involving no expense whatever for machinery, and of eventually producing a profit to the establishment. With the exception of a few old men still continued as sweepers, all the eastern workers were now called in, and every individual capable of being employed was provided with work, and placed under a system of superintendence easily organized *within the walls,* though all efforts had failed of rendering it effectual as long as they remained *without.*"

It appears that two branches for employing the female poor presented themselves to the Committee, namely, spinning, and platting of straw: on the former we find in the Report the following observations: "That the result of their exertions seemed clearly to prove, that the spinning of coarse linen yarn held out the greatest prospect of advantage to an Association, whose proceedings in this particular must ever be regulated by the utmost delicacy and caution." The exertions of the Committee being limited by the scantiness of their funds, "they made an immediate application to the Trustees of the Linen Board, by whom they were kindly assisted with a grant of 50 wheels and five reels; they also set apart a room in the Repository in Hawkins'-street, as a kind of sale-room, to which wheelwrights were requested to send any wheels they might have on hand, in the hope that *visiters, being struck with the want of them in the Establishment and with the air of cheerfulness and comfort which so remarkably characterizes the industrious spinners, might be induced to assist the Institution by donations of wheels.*"

" There was also another source of supply to which your Committee have peculiar gratification in adverting, namely, the formation of a Penny-a-week Society; a benevolent project set on foot by some ladies, for the express purpose of providing wheels for the Institution, and from which very material assistance was derived."

The manufacture of straw-plat, with the importance it appeared to possess, is thus noticed in the Report: " A school for instruction in this art had been formed, consisting of 127 young girls. The degree of proficiency they had acquired during only a short period of instruction, and even under a very imperfect system of management, made it advisable, in the opinion of your Committee, to give it the advantage of a more efficient superintendence under the care of a Sub-Committee appointed for the express purpose. The rapid improvement which took place in consequence of the regulations then adopted more than answered the most sanguine expectations formed respecting this manufacture: not only was mere manual dexterity acquired, but a spirit of emulation excited, and habits of cleanliness and order were established; besides which, a portion of mental instruction was daily imparted.

" In order that the system of management, with regard to this school, might be as complete as possible, a *Savings Bank* was introduced: by this means the trifle, which these little workers could afford to deposit weekly, was husbanded: and thus, in many instances, an industrious child was enabled to indulge in the honest pride of wearing clothes which had been partly paid for by the wages of superior skill and diligence. This system had also in other points of view the best effect: it gave the workers an idea of thrift, and a spirit of industry and independence; whilst it added to their comforts, and thus raised them in the scale of society. So great indeed was the change which manifested itself in the appearance, manners, and spirits of these children, that your Committee have often had the gratification, whilst attending strangers through the Institution, of hearing doubts expressed whether many of the young persons whom they saw in this department could ever have been *in the low state of actual mendicity :* thus effectually had a mild discipline and cheerful industry operated on their youthful minds, and so completely were the traces of the ' beggar's child' lost in those of the little active labourer. In the mean time, many of them became able to cover the expense of their maintenance by the produce of their industry; and it is not more extraordinary than true, that upwards of 100 children were enabled to earn their bread, in the straw-plat school alone, independent of the Institution; while many have gone into comfortable service.—A second School, consisting of 65 children, has since been formed, and is now fast approaching to a degree of skill which will probably ensure the same beneficial results."

It is also stated that 252 children belonging to other schools under the care of the Association, had been, in the course of the last year, either taken into the service of different individuals, or had left the Institution with their parents.

The *moral and religious instruction of the poor* also appears to have occupied the serious care of the Committee. They state that "*Sunday Schools* form a most interesting feature in their establishment, not only as they regard the younger branches, but adults also. They allowed no Sunday of the past year to go by, without providing for the due performance of divine service according to the rites of the respective Churches; and care was taken that adults as well as children should have an opportunity of receiving religious instruction from teachers of their own persuasion: and several of these poor people have been thereby led to become constant attendants on a sacred duty they had previously neglected, and have been often seen to shed tears at the serious mention of that Name which had scarcely ever before been sounded in their ears but in the curse of impiety or the cant of imposture."

The Committee, in continuing their unremitted attention to the employment of the poor, observed another important advantage arising from such institutions; namely, "That the pauper, who cannot procure better bread, is obliged to work in them in preference to being idle; by which means the community becomes naturally and legitimately informed of the lowest rate at which labour can be obtained; whereby individuals or companies may be induced to undertake projects perhaps highly advantageous to the country, and which, but for the facilities thus afforded, might never have been attempted."

The *spinning of flax* appears to be regarded as the staple employment in this Institution. At first the number of wheels was deficient, owing to a scantiness of the funds; but enough were afterwards obtained to employ all the females in the Establishment who were capable of using them.

"Subsequently to this period, two gentlemen of enterprize and intelligence set on foot an establishment for spinning fine woollen yarns, for the manufacture of *poplins:* the facilities which this Institution offered, in the low price of labour, afforded an opportunity of making trial of a manufacture which now promises to be very advantageous. To answer the demand arising from this experiment, nearly 200 of the most expert spinners were selected from the Establishment, who are now earning a comfortable and independent subsistence by their industry. And an assurance was given, that in a short time a further number would be taken, and provided for in a similar manner. Such a fact as this is the more gratifying, as it goes strongly to prove the value of a system which, by its stated employments, makes the transition so easy from *beggary and idleness to useful industry*. And thus the Institution itself has assumed rather the appearance of a regular *workshop* than an *almshouse*. Under such a system, the Committee ask, Is there any thing which can tend to relax foresight, or weaken a reliance on their own exertion among the poor under their charge? is there any thing beyond the prospect of a bare support, earned by honest industry, which can tempt them to remain in this Establishment? or, lastly, is there any thing which, during their continuance in it, can tend to cut them off from society, its business, its cares, or its intercourse? In support of the obvious reply, one general fact may be adduced as conclusive,—that whereas the number in the Institution, as recorded in the last Annual Report, was 2930, including children; a similar return at the present day amounts to only 1106, of which number not more than 355 individuals appeared on the books at the commencement of the present year."

Two new kinds of manufacture are stated to have been lately set on foot in the Institution, concerning which no correct judgment can yet be formed : one is *lace-making*, in which a few children are employed ; the other, that of manufacturing a coarse kind of *blanketing*, or coverlids for beds, from cows' hair.

"The boys have been principally employed in *making nets*, by which they have in a great degree covered the expense of their maintenance. This work is in itself perhaps of no great importance, not being an employment by which in after-life they are likely to gain a subsistence; but the *principle* of calling forth exertion and enforcing habits of industry is so *valuable*, that the Committee hope that even these simple means may effect much good."

In spite, however, of all the vigilance of the Committee, and of their utmost endeavours to keep the poor, who were the objects of their care, in activity, defects of considerable magnitude were discovered, and abuses crept in, which were evidently beyond their power to remedy. A morbid mass of indolence, if the simile may be allowed, still lurked under the healthful exterior of regular industry, which not only grew constantly more corrupt in itself, but became enlarged by the noxious influence of example. It was therefore deemed expedient to introduce such a system of occupation, as, while it included every individual, and demanded from all a proper degree of exertion, was calculated to infuse life and vigour into the slothful and inert, and thereby to effect a most important change. The impostor, now brought to a proper test, tacitly confessed what will frequently elude the strictest investigation, and left the Establishment to seek a refuge in those haunts where artifice and idleness are less exposed to detection.

"During the infancy of the Institution, the distribution of food formed no feature in the plans adopted; all allowances were expressly made in *money:* this practice, however sound in principle, and consistent with the common order of things, it afterwards appeared expedient to abandon. It will be recollected that an epidemic, brought on by want and improper food, during a period of scarcity, was spreading fatally among the lower orders: it was therefore important, in an Institution such as this, to check its inroads, if possible, by means of a wholesome and nutritious diet."

Carts were accordingly sent round the town to collect from the benevolent inhabitants such broken meat as they were disposed to contribute for the use of the poor, which was to be dispensed from a public kitchen: thus the food that had before been given, sometimes perhaps too lavishly, to a few individuals, now afforded, with the addition of bread, soup, and some other nutritive ingredients, many comfortable meals to a much larger number of persons.

The Committee perceived, however, that by *giving* a stated allowance of food to all classes within the Institution, whether *employed* or *unemployed*, they had fallen into an error, which they afterwards corrected. It appeared that indolence, finding the mere cravings of nature satisfied, was content to sit out the day in listless torpor, while industry no longer felt that brisk stimulus to diligence, which *necessity*, wisely intended by the Author of Good to be the chief spring of human exertion, can alone supply. It was accordingly determined, "That no persons, capable of being employed, should for the future receive a *gratuitous* allowance of food; but that the wages of such persons should be paid in money only: and in order to secure to them the power of obtaining a sufficiency of wholesome food for the day at a cheap rate, the privilege of *purchasing* rations from the public kitchen was granted to all the individuals of this class who might choose to avail themselves of it. At the same time an exception to the rule was made in favour of the learners of any new employment, and of those who were incapable of labour. These rations, consisting of 3 pounds 4 ounces of wholesome food, were to be purchased at the public kitchen at the price of one penny; being something less than their cost to the Institution. They have been since increased to four pounds, and distributed twice a-day at a halfpenny each ration; which plan has been acted on ever since, and found to answer, most generally, the objects proposed by its adoption. In the mean time a considerable reduction in the expense of providing it has been effected."

A gratuitous allowance of rations, together with the sum of two-pence, was given to all persons belonging to the Establishment who chose to attend at church on Sunday. By this means all pretence for begging on that day was removed; while an opportunity was afforded of adding something to the earnings of those labourers, who, being on a very low rate of wages, might require some little assistance to meet the price of lodging, which is necessarily high in the capital."

The premises, in which these great operations of industry are carried on, are described as being spacious and well calculated for the purposes of a vast *workshop*. They are conveniently situated in Hawkins'-street, in a central part of the city, offering no annoyance to any of the superior classes of inhabitants; and are held at the moderate rent of 300*l.* per annum, payable by monthly instalments. The scene of activity which this Establishment presents is continually visited by the rich and benevolent, and thus a general interest is kept alive in the public mind; to which circumstance, the Committee are of opinion, a very considerable portion of the funds may be attributed.

" To this asylum the poor and the indigent are freely admitted, but with strict adherence to the following principles: The adult is received within its walls; not to eat the bread of idleness: his meal awaits him, but his own *industry* can alone give him the title to enjoy it; and even then the quality is coarse, and offers no temptation save what the charm of independence may throw around it. His child may there spend the day in the schools of industry or instruction, but at night he returns with his parent to a home which the wages of industry now enable them to call *their own.* The doors are open, with the same intent, to the orphan during the day; and at night, no longer uncertain where to lay his head, he claims shelter with the family whom this Association remunerates for his adoption."

We would ask, Can any system be more judiciously arranged, or more happily contrived, to call forth a spirit of industry and forethought in those poor unfortunate beings who are the objects of its care, and who now possess the means of restoration to their proper station in society?

It now only remains to notice the *means* by which the Committee were enabled to succeed in the grand and arduous undertaking already described. It will be remembered that no compulsory power of the law exists in Ireland, as it respects any provision for the poor: it was necessary, therefore, to have recourse to voluntary contributions; and this may justly be considered as having been the most difficult and discouraging part of the business. The Committee set out with the belief that a charity which had established such powerful claims on the liberality of the public, would require the employment of *gratuitous aid alone* for the purpose of its support. They felt that the pure cause in which they had engaged was worthy of that aid, and were averse to the idea of allowing a *hired* agency to usurp the place of exertions springing solely from motives of benevolence. It was determined, therefore, that a number of gentlemen residing in different parts of the town should be solicited to collect in their own immediate neighbourhood; and that the clergy of all religious persuasions should be requested to advocate the cause of the Institution among their congregations. And the Committee themselves agreed to wait, by deputation or otherwise, on those individuals whose rank or situation entitled them to this mark of respect.

The Lord Mayor of Dublin kindly allowed the Committee to place his name at the head of their Finance Committee, and gave them permission to hold their meetings at the Mansion-House; a privilege which was attended with the best effects. By their exertions, funds were at first raised sufficient to enable the Committee to carry forward, to a certain extent, the business of the Institution. But, within a month after the commencement, the funds not coming in as was expected, the Committee, with a weekly expenditure of 87*l*. and having incurred a debt of 800*l*. had no alternative left but to permit the Institution to fall, or to become themselves personally responsible, to a certain extent, for the payment of such debts as would be unavoidably incurred by a further prosecution of their labours. Feeling, however, a sort of "fascination" concerning the cause they had undertaken, it was not possible for them to desert it; the interests of the poor objects they were daily communing with had been too intimately interwoven with their sympathies to allow them to abandon this great charity, and throw back their charge, reformed as many were, upon wretchedness and ruin: they knew that difficulties, almost hopeless, had before been surmounted; they felt assured that the sympathy of a generous public must again revive, and they resolved to "cast their bread upon the waters," in a firm reliance, that "after many days it would return."

The funds raised for carrying on this important work still continued precarious until the beginning of April, 1819; when a General Meeting was convened, and the state of the Institution laid before the Subscribers. It happened, fortunately, at this juncture, that the debt, now amounting to about 1000*l*. was cleared off by the receipts of a public entertainment, which enabled the Committee to come forward with greater confidence. From experience, they were now enabled to prove that the object for which the Association was formed was *perfectly attainable;* and at a price which must be esteemed low, when divided among the number of houses which the city contains. The Committee professed their readiness to continue their efforts in the service of the public, so long as funds should be forthcoming; and having discharged all arrears, they claimed that liberal and steady support which alone would enable them to carry on the business of the Institution, without incurring fresh debts. In consequence of this statement, a resolution was passed, authorising the Committee to suspend their labours, whenever the necessity should again arise of incurring debt. The meeting was then adjourned for a fortnight; and the citizens were in the mean time requested to consider of the best means of establishing some permanent and effective mode of collection. The sensation thus excited was unexpectedly great; and at the next meeting the Committee were directed to employ persons for the purpose of making immediate application to *every householder* in the city, in order to ascertain his sentiments on the subject, and the sum he might be willing to subscribe in support of the Institution; a measure which was forthwith carried into effect, and which has been the means of since bringing in supplies to a considerable amount.

Towards the latter end of the summer a more general and lively interest was evinced by the public, serving to prove that something of a steady warmth of feeling had been excited, widely differing from that doubtful and casual support which had before been so discouraging to the friends of the Institution. Several ladies now benevolently came forward, some to form societies for the purpose of contributing small sums weekly; some to collect funds for the purpose of providing wheels; and others to make and dispose of toys and other small articles, by the sale of which the general fund might be augmented.

The amount of expenditure for one year, ending Dec. 31, 1819, is stated at 12,462*l.* leaving a balance in hand in favour of the Institution of 898*l.* 5*s.*

Respecting the Flax department, the Committee observe, that " Since the month of September last, 4 ton 15 cwt. 2 qrs. and 24lb. had been purchased at the price of 283*l.* 5*s.* 8*d.*; the cost of spinning and dressing, with repair of wheels, &c. was 252*l.* 5*s.* 3*d.*; the produce of sales and value of stock on hand, 377*l.* 10*s.* 9*d.*; and the loss on the whole transaction, 158*l.* 0*s.* 2*d.* Unfavourable as this result may at first sight appear, a reflecting mind will probably see ample reason to admit that much good has, nevertheless, been effected; for let it be remembered *that every shilling by which the produce of the labour exceeds the cost of the raw material is just so much gain to the community.* As beggars in the streets, the persons in question obtained their entire support by idleness; as paupers in this institution, though they may not have entirely maintained themselves, they have contributed considerably to that support; consequently, in this view alone, a nuisance has been suppressed, and at the same time expense has been saved to the public, to the amount of the return arising from the *labour* of the paupers. And here a very satisfactory reason may be assigned why associations of this nature can never be expected to advance much beyond this point; *because the moment they have brought their workers to such a degree of dexterity, and to such habits of industry, as may enable them to earn their own subsistence, the managers must expect to lose them, and forfeit, as it respects the Institution, all the benefit which might be derived from their improved skill: the object of the poor in such institutions will ever be, under a sound system, to escape from it, and to obtain better and more independent bread elsewhere.* This Institution aims only at rendering those under its care qualified to leave it, and does not expect profit from their labour.

"In elucidation of this subject, the Committee refer to the number of expert spinners taken from the Institution, as before stated; and also to the whole class of straw-platters, who have found employment out of the Establishment as soon as they became expert; that is, at the very period when their labours might be expected to return a profit, and pay, in some measure, the expense of their instruction."

The Committee, then, have to congratulate the public and themselves in their having been happily instrumental in reforming the morals of the lower classes, so as to produce an evident diminution of crime, particularly among the class of juvenile delinquents; and this important fact has not only been recorded by the police magistrates, but has been expressly and repeatedly adverted to from the Judicial Bench, in terms highly gratifying to all parties.

The Committee, before they close their Report, repeat with much earnestness a warning which they had before given to the inhabitants, *to abstain from the practice of giving alms in the streets; a practice by which the success of the Institution had been materially checked, and its best effects counteracted.* In conclusion they state, that "if funds sufficient for carrying on the business of the Institution be regularly supplied; if alms be in any considerable degree withheld from beggars in the streets, or moderate powers to prevent successful imposture be granted to the Police; they entertain the most confident opinion that *street-begging will be at an end in the city of Dublin.* On the whole, they conceive that there is much ground for hope. The advance of the Institution in improvement and in public estimation has been progressive: and though it may sometimes have appeared stationary, *it has been at no period retrograde.* Experience has been found to be the best means of allaying many doubts and fears, and it has afforded the best answer to several objections which impeded the early progress of the Institution: most of the obstacles which appeared to justify the apathy of some, and certainly chilled the ardour of many, are now happily removed. Let us hope then, say they, that those checks to its growth have operated in establishing its strength, and that henceforth its steady advances towards maturity will more than compensate the struggles of its infancy."

In presenting the British public with the foregoing analysis of the Second Report of the "Association for the Suppression of Medicity in Dublin," the compiler has to apologize for the necessity he has been under of abridging several parts of that most interesting document, in order to compress it within the prescribed limits of his work. He trusts, however, that enough of actual experiment appears, to prove that *Mendicity*, the most alarming disease of civil society, is not *incurable*. And, when it is considered that so wise and enlightened a system of political economy as the preceding, has been brought to maturity, in the course of two years, in a part of the empire labouring under many disadvantages with respect to the lower classes of society, we might, perhaps, be allowed to express our surprise that benevolent persons in this country should not yet have been animated to imitate the patriotic example thus held out by our friends of Dublin, were it not for the too well remembered fact, that our Poor-Laws allow us no choice either to *give* or to *withhold* contributions from the parish poor; and that when we have satisfied the demands of the law in their behalf, we seem to have done for them all that it is in our power to do.

ON THE MODE OF PREPARING AND APPLYING

Oyster-Shells for Manure.

AFTER the mention of this profitable employment for the Poor, in the preceding article, it may not be unacceptable to the reader to be informed of the actual details of the process for preparing and applying the oyster-shells.

The instruments for pounding or pulverising these shells may be constructed somewhat like the *rammers* used by paviers, and shod with iron.

By an extract from a letter of Mr. BLAKIE, of *Holkham*, to Sir JOHN SINCLAIR, dated 18th Sept. 1818, and since published, it appears that this manure was tried in 1816, with complete success, on the farm of Mr. COKE, a well-known agriculturist of eminence. "The first experiment was made on a hungry, light, sandy soil, which had been cleaned for turnips. The oyster-shell powder was drilled in the usual way, upon 27-inch ridges, at the rate of 40 bushels per acre, without any other manure: it was slightly covered with earth, and the turnip-seed sown upon it. Another part of the same field, equal in quality, was manured with farm-yard dung, at the rate of 8 tons per acre, managed and sown with turnip-seed, as before, no other manure having been applied. The turnips proved a good crop on both pieces; nor was there any perceptible difference in the bulk, but the produce was not *weighed*. The succeeding barley-crop was equally good on both, as was the crop of clover."

"The second experiment," says Mr. Blakie, "was tried with *wheat*, upon a one-year's clover layer, in a light gravelly loam; the wheat being sown after ploughing. The oyster-shell powder, at the rate of 4 cwt. per acre, was drilled in with the seed; and in another part of the field (the quality of the soil being the same) rape-cake dust was drilled with the wheat at the same rate per acre as the shell powder. The crop of wheat was good in both instances; nor was there any perceptible difference, though the produce was not thrashed separately."

The same writer gives it as his opinion, that oyster-shell manure is likely to answer well for gardens, particularly when raked in with onions and other small seeds; and he thinks it may prove beneficial to use it as a top-dressing for grass-plats, to destroy moss and prevent worms from casting.

As this manure is obviously not less efficacious than the more common sorts, it derives a *genuine superiority* from the *portableness* of its nature. The farmer and gardener would, it is presumed, be very ready, after a fair trial, to adopt it on this ground. Its value, in the estimation of the philanthropist, consists in the converting of a useless article into a means of employing numbers of poor destitute families; and the residents in large cities, who are aware of the prodigious quantities of these shells that are collected and thrown into heaps in the ordinary receiving-places of city rubbish, need not be informed that they are commonly looked upon as worse than useless after being deposited there.

THE following "Account" though its date be less recent than that of the preceding one from Dublin presents such a variety of useful hints for the employment of the POOR, that we are persuaded the philanthropist will derive much practical information from its several details.

An Account of an Establishment for meliorating the Condition of the POOR *at* MUNICH; *together with a detail of various Public Measures which were adopted and carried into effect for putting an end to Mendicity, and for introducing Order and useful Industry among the indigent Inhabitants of Bavaria. By* BENJAMIN COUNT OF RUMFORD. *Extracted from his* " *Essays political, economical, and philosophical.*" Printed in London, 1797.

———

THE name of this distinguished character will long be deservedly held in public estimation for the improvements which he has introduced into society in the construction of chimneys, fire-places, and stoves, to the great saving of fuel, and the increase of the warmth and comfort of rooms. Also, for his approved methods of preparing a great variety of cheap, wholesome, and nutritive sorts of food for the poor.

Previously to Count Rumford's grand attempt to improve the condition of the Poor in Bavaria, namely, about the year 1790, *mendicity* had arrived at a most alarming height in that country (particularly in Munich, its capital). The number of itinerant beggars, of both sexes and of all ages, as well foreigners as natives, that were to be seen in all directions, was quite incredible. These, while they lived a life of indolence and the most shameless debauchery, levied contributions upon the industrious inhabitants, not merely by begging, but by private theft and public robbery; and so great was their impudence, and so persevering their importunity, that it was almost impossible to cross the streets without being attacked, and *absolutely forced* to satisfy their clamorous demands. Nor were these beggars, in general, such as, from age or bodily infirmities, were unable to earn their livelihood by their labour; but they were, for the most part, strong, sturdy persons, who, lost to every sense of shame, had embraced the profession of mendicity from choice, and not from necessity. These beings had recourse to the most diabolical arts and horrid crimes,* in prosecuting their infamous trade. Young children were stolen from their parents and their eyes put out, or their tender limbs broken or distorted, and they were thus exposed to public view, in order to excite compassion; while every species of artifice was made use of to agitate the sensibility of the humane and charitable, and to extort contributions from them.

These daring outrages on the good order of society were no longer to be borne. Several attempts had been made for suppressing mendicity, and, as they had all failed in succession, the public began to consider the case as a hopeless one. At this important crisis the energies of Count Rumford's active mind were put in requisition; and the expedient which immediately presented itself to him, as carrying with it any rational hope of curing these inveterate disorders, was *employment*. To furnish employment, however, for an immense number of idle unprincipled beggars, unused, if not disinclined to work, was to be regarded as a most difficult, if not an impracticable attempt. To trust raw materials in the hands of persons of this description, certainly required great caution; but to attempt to produce a radical change in their morals, manners, and habits, was to be considered more in the light of the visionary scheme of a warm enthusiast than the cool design of a practical politician.

"With persons of mendicant habits," says the Count, "it is easy to be conceived that precepts, admonitions, and punishments, would be alike unavailing. But where precepts fail, *habits* may sometimes be successfully superinduced to *counteract* habits. To make vicious and abandoned persons happy, it has generally been supposed necessary, *first*, to make them *virtuous;* but why not reverse this order: why not *first* make them *happy*, and then virtuous? If happiness and virtue be inseparable, the end will as certainly be obtained by the one method as by the other; and it is undoubtedly much easier to contribute to the happiness and

---

* As a proof of the improvement which has happily taken place in the morals of the lower orders of the people in BAVARIA, since the plans of reformation adopted by COUNT RUMFORD, we are informed by a "Friend," who visited Munich at the end of the year 1819, that in Bavaria, which contains a population of 2,500,000 inhabitants, there have been only *two* persons *condemned to death in the course of the last five years;* and that even on these the sentence of condemnation had not been confirmed!!!

We have to lament that this short and striking notice of the result of so mild and rational a system of jurisprudence in a foreign country, should serve only to remind us of the consequences resulting from the sanguinary nature of our own penal code; namely, *the certain continuance and increase of crime.*

comfort of persons *in a state of poverty and misery*, than to reform their morals by admonition or punishment."*

Deeply struck with the importance of this truth, the Count took all his measures accordingly. Every thing was done with a view to render the poor, whose cause he was about to undertake, comfortable and happy. He considered what circumstance in life (after the necessaries of food and raiment were supplied) would contribute most to *comfort*, and he decided that it was *cleanliness*.

The influence of cleanliness is so extensively felt, that it reaches even to the brute creation.—Many sorts of quadrupeds lick themselves and their young by way of cleansing their bodies. And the feathered tribes: with what care and attention do they wash themselves and arrange their plumage! What an elegant neatness, amounting almost to moral expression, in their appearance! So, amongst human beings, cleanliness promotes health, whilst it increases comfort; and so great is its influence that it may be said to extend even to the moral character. Our author gives it as his opinion, that " as virtue never dwelt long with filth and impurity, so there never was a person scrupulously attentive to cleanliness, who was a consummate villain."

The objects of this benevolent care and attention had certainly been used to live in a condition the most wretched and deplorable that can be conceived. They had dwelt in miserable hovels, in the midst of vermin and every kind of filth: they had slept in the streets, or under hedges, half naked, and exposed to all the inclemencies of the weather; and, by habit, they were grown insensible to their wretchedness. So that it became necessary to awaken their perceptions, by producing a contrast between their former situation and the one that was intended for them. Every thing was therefore done with a view of making them sensible of their present comfort; and strict orders were given that the utmost *cleanliness* and *neatness* should appear around them, at the same time that they were furnished with every thing necessary to their condition.

The pleasure which the COUNT eventually derived from these benevolent measures may be more easily conceived than described. " Would to GOD (he exclaims) that my success might encourage others to follow my example! If it were generally known how *little*

---

* The truth of this remark has been recently exemplified in the system of reform introduced by ELIZABETH FRY and her friends, amongst the most abandoned female criminals in Newgate. By *kindness*, judiciously tempered with moral restraint; by *employment*, happily united with *moral* and *religious instruction;* and by rules, the observance of which was not to be dispensed with, a most surprising reformation has been wrought among the very outcasts of society.

trouble and how *little* expense are required *to do much good*, the heartfelt satisfaction which arises from relieving the wants and promoting the happiness of our fellow-creatures is so great, that, I am persuaded, acts of the most essential charity would be no longer rare; and the mass of misery among mankind would, consequently, be much lessened."

The proceedings of this philanthropist, in bringing about his plan of reform in society, are described by him as having been eminently successful. For the proofs of the fact, he appeals to the flourishing state of the establishment, the orderly and peaceable demeanour of the poor employed in it, their cheerfulness, their industry, their manifest desire to excel, and even the very expression of their countenances.

Strangers who visited them (and there were very few who passed through Munich who did not take that trouble) could not sufficiently express their admiration at the air of happiness and contentment which reigned throughout every part of this extensive Establishment; they could hardly be persuaded that among those whom they saw so cheerfully engaged in the interesting scenes of industry, by far the greater number had been, five years before, the most miserable and worthless of beings—common beggars in the streets.—But it is time now to proceed to notice the

MEANS TAKEN FOR COLLECTING THE VAGRANTS.

Before this vast multitude of itinerant beggars could be set to work, it became necessary to collect them together, and to examine them.

It appears that COUNT RUMFORD'was *Chamberlain, Privy Counsellor of State,* and *Lieutenant-General* in the service of the ELECTOR PALATINE, the reigning DUKE of BAVARIA; that he enjoyed the confidence of this Prince; and acted, in all his plans for the improvement of the condition of the Poor, under the immediate authority, and with the approbation of his Sovereign. Being thus armed with the full powers of the government, a plan was formed by the COUNT of *employing the Army in clearing the country of these beggars, thieves, and vagabonds.* This was certainly a bold measure, and such as, in Great-Britain, (where the people are jealous of their liberties,) no Minister of State would dare to attempt; but under a government less free than *our own,* it proved a most judicious and salutary step.

To prevent disputes, however, between the military and the civil authorities, and to preserve peace and harmony between themselves and the inhabitants, the troops were strictly enjoined to behave with the utmost respect and deference towards magistrates, and other persons in civil authority; to conduct themselves towards the peasants, and the inhabitants generally, in the most peaceable and friendly manner: to retire to their quarters very early in the evening; and, above all, cautiously to avoid all occasions of dispute and quarrel. They were ordered to be very diligent, while performing their daily patroles from one station to another, in apprehending all thieves and vagabonds, and in delivering them over to the civil magistrates.

To convince the public, too, that it was not intended to carry this measure into execution by military force *alone* (which might have rendered it odious), the magistrates, were requested, in company with the field officers of the garrison, to assist in the execution of the *first and most difficult part of the undertaking*, that of *arresting the beggars*.

These preliminary arrangements having been made, and a large building having been prepared for receiving and employing these people, *New-year's day* was chosen, as the most favourable time for beginning so novel and arduous an undertaking.

That day had been considered in Bavaria, from time immemorial, as peculiarly set apart for *giving alms*; and the beggars, of course, never failed to be out and ready for such an occasion. It was commanded, therefore, that early in the morning of the first of January, 1790, the officers and non-commissioned officers of three regiments of infantry at MUNICH should be stationed in the different streets, where they were to wait for further orders.

The COUNT having, in the mean time, assembled in his apartments the field officers, and all the chief magistrates of the town, accquainted them with his intention to proceed, that very morning, to the execution of his plan, and requested their prompt assistance.

This they most readily assented to, and the united party immediately sallied into the street: the Count being accompanied by the Chief Magistrate of the town, and each of the field officers by an inferior magistrate.

In this order they dispersed themselves through the town; and being aided by the soldiers, who had been waiting for orders, they so thoroughly cleared the streets of beggars *in less than an hour*, that not one was any longer to be seen.

The arrested persons were then conducted to the *town-hall*, where their names, and places of abode, if they had any, were inscribed in printed lists, provided for that purpose; after which they were dismissed to their lodgings, with directions to repair the next day to the newly-erected *Military Workhouse* in the *Au*. They were informed at the same time that a Commission should be immediately instituted for inquiring into their circumstances, and for granting to the destitute, who were unable to work, such weekly allowances of money, as they should stand in need of.

An ADDRESS to the inhabitants and citizens of Munich, in the form of an Appeal, was next printed and circulated, stating that *morality* and *religion*, as well as the public honour and safety, had called aloud for the extirpation of this evil, which, though habit had rendered it familiar, was horrid and disgusting in every view. That *idleness* and *mendicity* (those pests of society), acquiring vigour from success, had hitherto, in that city, triumphed over all the weak attempts which had been made to restrain them.

That the dreadful consequences which would ensue had been obvious, when hordes of vagrants live in idleness, without any settled abode, concluding every day with schemes for plundering or imposing upon the public the next. That the children belonging to this banditti of beggars were regularly trained, from their infancy, in all those infamous practices of fraud and imposture, which were carried on systematically to a most alarming extent.

That great numbers of these children grew up to die under the hands of the executioner; the only instruction which they had received from their parents having been how to cheat and deceive the most expertly. That the records of the Courts of Justice would show, in innumerable instances, that early habits of idleness and beggary had been a preparation for the gallows; and it had been ascertained that among the numerous thefts daily committed in the capital, the greater number of them were perpetrated by persons who stole into houses, *under the pretext of asking charity* That no crime was too horrible or shocking for these wretched people to commit, who were accustomed to laugh alike at the laws of GOD and of man; that, in short, nothing in heaven or on earth was too holy, not to be profaned by them without scruple.

The Address then cautioned the Public against the *indiscriminate or injudicious dispensation of Alms,* which had been in reality, the chief source of so great an evil. It has been asserted that those who lavish their alms by mistaken compassion, upon beggars, obstruct the relief of the really indigent poor, who frequently suffer the greatest distress and want, before they can bring themselves openly to solicit the assistance of the public. That those alms which encourage idleness and vice, and frustrate the exertions of industry, cannot be meritorious, or acceptable to GOD; and that no maxim is less founded in truth than that *" the merit of the giver is not diminished by the unworthiness of the object."*

The citizens and inhabitants of the capital were therefore earnestly entreated, instead of giving further countenance to *mendicity,* by this misapplication of their well-meant charity, to contribute liberally towards a public fund, about to be vested in the hands of men of honour, judgment, and integrity; who would be responsible for the faithful application of all sums entrusted to their care, for the relief of the impotent, indigent, and really distressed Poor.

This Address, which was presented to all the heads of families in the city, and to many of them by the Count himself, who went round to the principal citizens for that purpose, was accompanied by printed blank lists, with proper headings, in which the inhabitants were requested to set down their names, places of abode, and the sums they chose to subscribe *monthly*, for the support of the proposed establishment, about to be instituted by the command of the Elector Palatine.

They were informed that these subscriptions, being *perfectly voluntary*, might be augmented or diminished at pleasure. As soon as the lists were all completed, they were collected and sorted, and regularly entered, according to the numbers of the houses of the subscribers, in sixteen general lists, answering to the sixteen subdivisions or districts of the city; and a copy of the general list of each district was given to the Commissary of the district.

The amount of the collection was then delivered by the Commissary to the Banker of the institution, and published every three months in the Gazette. But as there were some persons who, from modesty or other motives, did not choose to have it publicly known how much they gave in alms to the poor, a plan was adopted by which the contributions of these persons were entered under a feigned name, or by initials, motto, or device; and the receipt of the sums they gave, acknowledged in the Munich Gazette accordingly. Fixed *poor-boxes* were also placed in all the churches, and in most of the inns, coffee-houses, and places of public resort, for the reception of small sums.

All these voluntary contributions were placed at the discretion of a Committtee, consisting of the *President of the Council of War*, the *President of the Council of the Regency*, the *President of the Ecclesiastical Council*, and the *President of the Chamber of Finance*. And it was particularly stipulated that no part of the money thus contributed should ever be appropriated to the payment of salaries, gratuities, or rewards, to any of those persons who might be employed in carrying on the business of the Institution; but that the whole should be faithfully applied to the uses of the poor, either by employing them, or gratuitously supporting them: and that all persons whose aid was necessary in the affairs of the Institution, should be selected from among those who already received salaries sufficient for their maintenance, from other funds; or from those who, being in easy circumstances, were able, from motives of humanity, to make a voluntary tender of their services.—It will now be proper to return to the means taken for collecting the vagrants.

The first day of the year, as has been already stated, was fixed upon for commencing their arrest; and it is subsequently affirmed that though the whole number of the inhabitants of the city of

Munich does not probably amount to more than 60,000, even including the suburbs, above *ten thousand* vagabonds were actually arrested and delivered over to the civil magistrates. Not less than *two thousand six hundred* mendicants, natives and foreigners, were entered upon the lists in *one week*.

Two principal objects called for attention in making the arrangements for receiving these beggars: the first was, to furnish suitable employment for those who were able to work; and the second, to provide the necessary assistance or support for those who, from age, sickness, or other bodily infirmities, were unable to provide for themselves. A general system of police was likewise necessary to be established among them; and measures taken for reclaiming them, with a view of making them useful subjects.

ACCOMMODATIONS FOR THE VAGRANTS.

It is easy to conceive that so great a number of unfortunate beings, of all ages and both sexes, taken as it were out of their very element, and placed in a situation so perfectly new to them, could not fail to be productive of very interesting circumstances. "Would to GOD," exclaims the Count, "I were able to do justice to this subject! but no language can describe the affecting scenes to which I was a witness upon this occasion. The exquisite delight which a humane mind must feel upon seeing many hundreds of wretched beings awaking, from a state of misery and inactivity, as from a dream, and applying themselves with cheerfulness to the employments of useful industry; upon beholding the first dawn of placid content break upon a countenance covered with habitual gloom, and furrowed and distorted by misery; this is easier to be conceived than described."

A large and commodious building, pleasantly situated in the Au, was provided for their reception. It had formerly been a manufactory, but was subsequently deserted, and had been falling into ruin: this was now completely repaired, and in part rebuilt.

To the main building a large kitchen, with a spacious eating-room adjoining to it, and a commodious bake house, were added. Workshops were erected for carpenters, smiths, turners, and such other mechanics as were constantly wanted in the manufactory for making and repairing the machinery, and they were furnished with tools. Large halls were provided, with accommodation for spinners of hemp, of flax, of cotton, of wool, and of worsted; and adjoining to each hall a small room was fitted up for a clerk, or inspector of the work (*spin-schreiber*). This room, which was at the same time a store-room and counting-house, had a large window opening to the hall, through which the spinners were supplied with raw materials, delivered their yarn when spun, and received an order upon the cashier, signed by the clerk, for the amount of their labour.

Halls were likewise fitted up for weavers of woollens, for weavers of serges and shalloons, for linen-weavers, and for weavers of cotton goods and stockings. Workshops were provided for clothiers, cloth-shearers, dyers, and saddlers; and rooms for wool-sorters, wool-carders, and wool-combers, knitters, sempstresses, &c. Magazines were fitted up, as well for finished manufactures as for raw materials; and there were rooms for counting-houses, store-rooms for the kitchen and bakehouse, and dwelling-rooms for the inspectors and other officers who were lodged in the house.

A very spacious hall, 110 feet long, 37 feet wide, and 22 feet high, with many windows on both sides, was fitted up for a drying-room, in which tenters were placed for stretching out and drying *eight pieces of cloth at once*. This hall was so contrived as to serve for the dyer and the clothier at the same time. A fulling-mill was erected, upon a stream of water which runs by one side of the court round which the building stands; and adjoining to the fulling-mill were the dyer's shop and the wash-house.

In the course of this fitting up, even the external appearance of the building was attended to. It was handsomely painted, without as well as within; and pains were taken to give it an air of *elegance*. A large court in the middle of the building was handsomely paved, the ground before the building was levelled and covered with gravel, and the approach to it from every side was made easy and commodious. Over the principal door, or rather gate, was an inscription, denoting the use to which the building was appropriated; and in the passage leading into the court there was written in large letters of gold, upon a black ground, " *No Alms will be received here.*"

Inscriptions were also seen over all the doors upon the ground-floor, in large gold letters, as before, denoting the particular uses to which the different apartments were destined.

In this retreat the poor had a good warm dinner provided for them every day *gratis*, cooked and served up with all possible attention to order and cleanliness. A sufficient number of spinning-wheels &c. having been provided, together with an adequate stock of raw materials; there were materials and utensils for those who were able to work, and there were masters for those who required instruction; they were offered the most liberal pay, in money, for all the labour they performed, and received the kindest usage from every person belonging to the establishment, from the highest to the lowest. In this asylum for the indigent and unfortunate, no ill usage, no harsh language was permitted. During the five years that the establishment existed, not a blow was given to any one; not even to a child by his instructor.

As it was winter, fires were kept in every part of the building, from morning till night; and all the rooms were lighted up till nine o'clock in the evening. Every room and every stair-case was neatly swept and cleaned twice a-day; once early in the morning, before the people were assembled, and once while they were at dinner. Care was taken, by placing ventilators, and occasionally opening the windows, to keep the air of the rooms perfectly free from all disagreeable smells; and the rooms themselves were not only neatly whitewashed and fitted up, but care was taken to clean the windows very often, to cleanse the court-yard every day, and even to clear away the rubbish from the street in front of the building to a considerable distance on every side.

THE DIFFERENT SORTS OF EMPLOYMENT.

During the first three or four days that these poor people were assembled, it was not possible entirely to prevent confusion; there was, however, nothing like mutinous resistance among them; but their situation was so new to them, and they were so very awkward in it at the beginning, that it was difficult to bring them into any tolerable order. At length, however, by distributing them in the different halls, and assigning to each his particular place (the places being all distinguished by numbers), the inspectors and instructors were enabled to begin their operations.

As by far the greater number of them were totally unacquainted with every kind of useful labour, it was necessary to give them such work at first as was easy to be performed, and in which the raw materials were of little value; and it was intended to employ them by degrees, and as they became more expert, in manfacturing more valuable articles.

As *Hemp* is a very cheap commodity, and the spinning of hemp is easily learned, particularly when it is designed for very coarse and ordinary manufactures, 15.000 pounds weight of that article had been purchased in the *Palatinate*, and transported to *Munich*: and good spinners, as instructors, had been engaged, in readiness for the opening of the house.

Flax and *Wool* had been likewise provided, and some few good spinners of those articles engaged as instructors.

Those who understood any kind of work were placed in the apartments where that work was carried on; and the others being *classed* according to their sexes, and as much as possible according to their ages, were placed under the immediate care of the different instructors. By much the larger number were put to spinning hemp; others, and many of the young children from four to seven years of age, were taught to knit and to sew; and the most awkward of the men, particularly the old, the lame, and the infirm, were put to carding wool. Old women, whose sight was too weak to spin, or whose hands trembled with palsy, were required to spool yarn for the weavers; and young children, who were too weak to labour, were placed upon seats erected for that purpose round the rooms where the older children were working.

It was necessary to pay them a liberal, or rather high price for the little work they were able to perform at first, in order to keep up their spirits, and induce them to persevere with cheerfulness in acquiring more skill and address in their labour. It must be obvious, however, that no manufacture can possibly subsist long where exorbitant prices are paid for labour; and it was also to be expected that discontent would arise among the labourers upon *lowering* the prices which had been paid to them for any length of time. To obviate this inconvenience, as the manufacture of *hemp* was not intended to be carried on to any considerable extent, it was intended afterwards when the poor were taken from that employment and put to spinning wool, worsted, or cotton, to fix the price of labour in these last-mentioned manufactures at a reasonable rate.

Those who were employed in this HOUSE were expected to arrive at an appointed hour in the morning, which hour varied according to the season of the year: if they came too late, they were gently reprimanded; and if they persisted in being tardy, without being able to give a sufficient reason for not coming sooner, they were punished by being deprived of their dinner, which they otherwise received every day *gratis*.

MEANS TO ENCOURAGE INDUSTRY.

It has already been observed how necessary it was to encourage, by every possible means, a spirit of industry and emulation among these people. Though a liberal price was paid them for their labour, yet that alone was not enough to interest them sufficiently in the occupations in which they were engaged.

To give them a true spirit of persevering industry, it was necessary to inspire them with emulation; to awaken in them a dormant passion, the influence of which they had perhaps never yet experienced,—the love of honest fame. For this purpose rewards were necessary; and these were employed. Those who distinguished themselves by their application, their industry, or their address, were publicly praised and encouraged: they were brought forward, and placed in the most conspicuous situations; pointed out to strangers who visited the establishment; and particularly named and proposed as models for their associates to copy. A peculiar dress, a sort of uniform, for the establishment had been provided; which, though economical, was nevertheless handsome: and as this dress was bestowed upon those only who had distinguished themselves, it was soon looked upon as an honourable mark of approved merit, and served very powerfully to excite emulation among the competitors. "I doubt," says our author, "whether vanity in any instance ever surveyed itself with more self-gratulation than did some of these poor people when they put on their new dress."

"How necessary it is to be acquainted with the hidden springs of action which rule the heart, in order to be able to direct even the rudest of mankind! The human machine is intrinsically the same in all situations; and the only secret seems to be *how to put it in tune,* before we attempt to *play upon it.* When the jarring sounds of former vibrations are all stilled, and the instrument is reduced to order, it is then, and then alone, that the touch of a skilful master can produce a complete effect.

"Though every thing was done with a view to impress the minds of all who were employed in this establishment with such sentiments as might conduce to their becoming good and useful members of society (and in these attempts I was certainly successful beyond even my most sanguine expectations), yet my hopes were chiefly placed on the *rising generation.*

"The *children* therefore of the poor were the objects of my peculiar care and attention. In order to induce their parents to send them to the establishment, even before they were old enough to do any kind of work, they not only received their dinner *gratis,* on attending at regular hours, but each of them was paid *three creutzers* a-day, merely for being present while the others were at work. The young children were placed upon seats round the halls where the older children worked, in order to inspire them with a desire to do that which those older ones, apparently more favoured, more caressed, and more praised than themselves, were permitted to do, and of which they were obliged to be idle spectators. This scheme had the desired effect.

"As nothing is so tedious to a child as being obliged to sit still in the same place for a considerable time, and as the work which the other more favoured children were engaged in was light and easy, and appeared rather amusing than otherwise, being the spinning of hemp and flax merely, with light wheels turned with the foot, these children, who were obliged to be spectators of so busy and entertaining a scene, became uneasy in their situations, and jealous of those who were permitted to be more active; they consequently solicited, with the greatest importunity, to be permitted to work, and often cried most heartily if this favour was not instantly granted them.

"How sweet such tears were to me," says the Count, "can easily be imagined; and the joy which followed on their being permitted to descend from their benches, and mix with the working children below, was equally interesting with the solicitude with which they had demanded the favour."

These children were at first only furnished with a wheel, which they turned for several days with the foot, without being permitted to attempt any thing further. As soon as they were become dexterous in this simple operation, and habit had made it so easy and familiar to them that the foot could continue its motion mechanically without the assistance of the head; when they could go on with their work, even though their attention was employed upon something else, answer questions, and converse freely with those about them upon indifferent subjects, without interrupting or embarrassing the regular motion of the wheel, then, and not till then, they were furnished with hemp or flax, and were taught to spin.

When they had arrived at a certain degree of dexterity in spinning hemp and flax, they were allowed to spin wool; and this was always represented to them, and considered by them, as an honourable promotion. Upon this occasion they commonly received publicly some reward—a new garment, a pair of shoes, or perhaps the uniform of the establishment—as an encouragement to them to persevere in their industrious habits.

As constant application, however, to any employment, for too long a time, is apt to produce disgust, and in children might even prove detrimental to health, an hour of relaxation from work, from eight till nine o'clock in the forenoon, and another hour, from three till four o'clock in the afternoon, were allowed them; and these two hours were spent in a school, which, for want of room elsewhere in the house, was kept in the dining-hall. Here they were taught reading, writing, and arithmetic, by a schoolmaster who was engaged and paid for that purpose. Besides, as the children were not confined like prisoners in the House of Industry, but were all lodged in the town, with their parents or friends, they had many opportunities of recreating themselves, and taking exercise in the open air; not only on holidays, of which a very large number are kept in Bavaria, but also on working-days, in coming to and going from their place of employment.

Persons of a more advanced age, also, who worked in the house, were admitted into the school at their own request; but few of these seemed desirous of availing themselves of the permission. As to the children, they had no choice in the matter: those who belonged to the House were obliged to attend the school regularly every day, morning and evening. The school-books, paper, pens, and ink, were furnished at the expense of the institution.

THE ADULTS SEPARATED AND CLASSED.

To create a distinction, among the grown persons who worked in the House, between those who shewed dexterity and industry in the different manufactures in which they were employed, and those who did not, the best workmen were separated from the others, and formed into distinct classes; and separate apartments were even assigned to them. This separation was productive of great benefits; for, beside the spirit of emulation which it excited throughout the establishment, it afforded an opportunity of carrying on the different manufactures to considerably greater advantage. The most dexterous among the wool-spinners, for instance, were collectively employed upon such wool as was used in the fabrication of the finest goods; and thus an obvious disadvantage was avoided; which is, that in the manipulations of the wool, as particles of it are unavoidably dispersed about in all directions, while spinning, if the coarser wool were spun near the fine, it would mix with it, and greatly injure the manufacture. For a similar reason, it was necessary to separate the spinners of different-coloured wool; but as these precautions are well known to all manufacturers, we shall forbear to go into a further detail of them.

RAW MATERIALS.

The *Steward*, or *Store-keeper of raw materials*, as he is called, has, in addition to these, the care of all finished manufactures destined for sale. The former are kept in magazines, or store-rooms, of which he alone has the keys. The latter are kept in rooms set apart as stores, or shops; where they are exposed to public inspection for sale. To prevent abuses in the sale of these manufactures, their prices, which are regulated by the cost of the labour bestowed on them, and a certain rate per cent. added for the profits of the house are marked upon the goods; and these prices are never altered. A regular account, too, is kept of all, even the most inconsiderable articles, sold; in which not only is the commodity specified, with its quality, quantity, and price, but the name of the purchaser is entered, and the day of the month when the purchase was made.

The order observed by the steward or store-keeper, with regard to the delivery of the raw materials, is as follows: in the manufactures of wool, for instance, he delivers to the master clothier a certain quantity, commonly 100 pounds, of wool, of a certain quality and description, taken from a certain division or bin in the magazine, bearing a certain number, in order to its being sorted. And as a register is kept of the wool that is put into these bins from time to time, and as the lots of wool are always kept separate, it is perfectly easy at any time to determine when, and where, and from whom, the wool delivered to the sorter was purchased, and what was paid for it; and consequently to trace the wool from the flock where it grew to the cloth into which it was formed, and even to the person who wore it. And similar arrangements are adopted with regard to all the raw materials used in all the different manufactures.

The advantages arising from this orderly proceeding are sufficiently obvious. We need only observe that numberless abuses are thus prevented on the part of the persons employed in the various manufactures, and a ready means is afforded of detecting any frauds on the part of those from whom the raw materials were purchased.

The wool received by the master clothier is delivered by him to the wool-sorters to be sorted. And, to prevent frauds on the part of the wool-sorters, not only do they all work in the same room, under the immediate inspection of the master wool-sorter, but a certain quantity of each lot of wool is sorted in the presence of some one of the public officers belonging to the house, in order to ascertain how much per cent. is lost by the separation of the dirt and filth in sorting; and thus the due quantity of sorted wool of the different qualities which the sorter is obliged to deliver is determined.

But the great art of the woollen-manufactory lies in the *sorting of the wool.* If this be not attended to, that is to say, if the different kinds of wool which every fleece naturally contains be not carefully separated, and if each kind of wool be not employed for that purpose, and *that alone* for which it is *best calculated*, no woollen-manufactory can possibly be carried on to advantage.

In this establishment, each fleece is commonly divided into *five* or *six* different sorts of wool, by the sorters; and of these, some are employed for the *warp*, others for the *woof*, others for *combing*;

and that which is very coarse and indifferent, for mittens for peasants, or for the lists of broad-cloth, &c.

The wool, when sorted, is delivered back by the master clothier to the steward, who now places it in the *sorted wool magazine;* and it is here put into separate bins, according to its different qualities and destinations, in order to be delivered out for manufacture. As these bins are all numbered, and as the quality and destination of the wool lodged in each bin is always the same, it is sufficient, in speaking of it afterwards, as it passes through the hands of the different manfacturers, merely to mention its *number;* that is to say, *the number of the bin* from which it was taken, *in the sorted wool-magazine.*

FURTHER PARTICULARS CONCERNING THE

RAW MATERIALS.

As a more minute account of the various manipulations of wool, and the means used to prevent frauds, may not only be interesting to all who are curious in such matters, but prove of real use to those who may be engaged in similar undertakings, we extract the following detail from our Author on that subject :

From the magazine of sorted wool the master clothier receives the sorted wool again, in order to its being wolfed, greased, carded, and spun; which are done under his inspection, and then it is delivered into the store-room of woollen yarn. As woollen yarn he receives it again, and delivers it to the cloth-weaver. The cloth-weaver returns it in cloth to the steward. The steward delivers it to the fuller, the fuller to the cloth-shearer, the cloth-shearer to the cloth-presser, and the cloth-presser to the steward ; and by this last it is delivered into the military magazine, if destined for the army; if not, it is placed in the shop for sale. The master clothier is answerable for all the sorted wool he receives till he delivers it to the clerk of the wool-spinners; and all his accounts are settled with the steward once a-week. The clerk of the spinners is answerable for the carded and combed wool he received from the master-clothier till it is delivered in yarn into the store-room; and his accounts are likewise settled with the master clothier, and the clerk of the store-room (who is called the clerk of the controul), once a-week. The spinners' wages are paid by the clerk of the controul, upon the spin-ticket being produced, signed by the clerk of the spinners, in which ticket the quantity and quality of the yarn spun being specified, together with the name of the spinner, the weekly delivery of yarn by the clerk of the spinners into the store-room must answer to the spin-tickets received and paid by the clerk of the controul. And the more effectually to prevent frauds, each delivery of yarn to the clerk of the spinners is bound up in a separate bundle, to which is attached an abstract of the spin-ticket, in which abstract is specified the name of the spinner, the date of the delivery, the number of the spin-ticket, and the quantity and quality of the yarn.

This management not only facilitates the settlement of the weekly accounts between the clerk of the spinners and the clerk of the controul, when the former makes his weekly delivery of yarn into the store-room, but renders it easy also to detect any frauds committed by the spinners.

The wages of the spinners are regulated by the fineness of the yarn; that is, by the number of skeins, or rather knots, which they spin from a pound of wool. Each knot is composed of 100 threads; and each thread, or turn of the reel, is two Bavarian yards in length: and to prevent frauds in reeling, *clock-reels*, proved and sealed, are furnished by the establishment to all the spinners. It is possible, however, notwithstanding this precaution, for the spinners to commit frauds, by binding up knots containing a smaller number of threads than 100. It is true, they have little temptation to do so; for as their wages are in fact paid by the *weight* of the yarn delivered, and the number of knots serving merely to determine the *price by the pound* which they have a right to receive, any advantages they can derive from frauds committed in reeling are very trifling indeed: but trifling as they are, such frauds would, no doubt, sometimes be committed, were it not known that it is absolutely *impossible to escape detection.*

The clerk of the spinners, therefore, not only examines the yarn when he receives it, and counts the threads in any of the knots which appear to be too small, but the name of the spinner, with a note specifying the quantity of knots, accompanies the yarn into the store-room, and from thence to the spooler, by whom it is wound off: thus, any frauds committed in reeling cannot fail to be brought home to the spinner.

The bundles of carded wool delivered to the spinners, though they are called pounds, are not exact pounds. They contain each as much more than a pound, as is necessary, allowing for wastage in spinning, to make the yarn, after it is spun, weigh a pound. If the yarn is found to be wanting in weight, a deduction is made from the wages of the spinner; which deduction, to prevent frauds, amounts to a trifle more than the value of the yarn found wanting.

FRAUDS IN OTHER DEPARTMENTS PREVENTED.

Frauds in weaving are prevented by delivering the yarn to the weavers by weight, and receiving the cloth by weight from the loom. In the other operations of the manufacture, such as fulling, shearing, pressing, &c. no frauds are to be apprehended.

Similar precautions are taken to prevent frauds in the linen, cotton, and other manufactures carried on in the house; and so effectual are the means adopted, that during more than five years since the establishment was instituted, no one fraud of the least consequence has been discovered, the evident impossibility of escaping detection in those practices having prevented the attempt. Besides, it has always been so contrived as to make one operation a check upon another, as well as to render all the persons employed in the various departments of this extensive manufactory *personally responsible* for all frauds and neglects committed in the different branches of which they have the oversight.

To show that the regulations are intrinsically good, our Author is of opinion that it is sufficient to refer to the flourishing state of the establishment, to its growing reputation, to its extensive connections, which reach even to foreign countries, to the punctuality with which all its engagements have been fulfilled, to its unimpeached credit, and to its growing wealth.

Notwithstanding all the disadvantages under which this institution laboured in its *infant state,* Count RUMFORD informs us that the net profits arising from it during the six years which it existed (previously to his publishing an account of it) amounted to above 100,000 *florins,* after the expenses of every kind, salaries, wages, repairs, &c. had been deducted; and that the business had so much increased in consequence of the increased demands for clothing for the troops, that the amount of the orders received and executed within the preceding year did not fall much short of *half a million of florins.*

He appears to be of opinion, that, in forming establishments, public or private, for giving employment to the poor, it will always be indispensably necessary so to manage as to secure to them a *fair* price for all the labour they perform. The labourers should not be *over-paid,* for that would be opening a door for abuse; but they ought to be liberally paid for their work, and *above all they ought never to be allowed to be idle for want of employment.* The sort of employment will depend much upon local circumstances, on the habits of the poor, the kinds of work they are acquainted with, and the facility with which an equitable price may be obtained for the articles they manfacture.

He seems to prefer *extensive* establishments for employing the poor to *smaller* ones, where they can be conveniently formed;

because the quantity of yarn spun by large numbers of spinners will always be sufficient to give work to a large number of weavers of different kinds of cloth and stuff: and it may be expected that, in this case, a market for all the various sorts of yarn would generally be certain; whereas, in a small establishment, circumscribed and confined to the limits of a single village or parish, it might, perhaps, be difficult to find a good market for the yarn spun by the poor.

Benevolent individuals, or small bodies of men, desirous of furnishing employment for the poor, must, however, content themselves with making such arrangements for this purpose as their circumstances may allow and their means command.

EFFECTS PRODUCED BY EMPLOYING THE POOR.

Notwithstanding the awkwardness of these poor people when they were first taken out of the streets of Munich, the facility with which they acquired address in their various employments was very remarkable, and much exceeded our Author's expectation. But what was quite surprising, and at the same time interesting in the highest degree, was the apparent and rapid change which was produced in their manners, and even in the very air of their countenances, after they had become accustomed to their new situations. The kind usage they had met with, and the comforts they had enjoyed, seemed to have softened their hearts, and awakened in them sentiments as new and surprising to themselves as they were interesting to those about them.

Their melancholy gloom of misery, and air of uneasiness and embarrassment, disappeared by little and little from their countenances, and were succeeded by a timid dawn of cheerfulness, rendered most exquisitely interesting by an expression of silent gratitude which no language can describe.

" In the infancy of this establishment [observes the Count], when these poor creatures were first brought together, I used to visit them very frequently, to speak kindly to them, and encourage them; and I seldom passed through the halls where they were at work, without being a witness to the most moving scenes.

" Objects formerly the most miserable and wretched, whom I had seen for many years as beggars in the streets; young women, perhaps the unhappy victims of seduction, who, having lost their reputation, and being turned adrift on the world, without a friend and without a home, had been reduced to the necessity of begging to sustain a miserable existence; now recognised me as their benefactor, and, with tears dropping fast from their cheeks, continued their work in the most expressive silence.

" If they were asked what was the matter with them, their answer was ' nichts' (nothing); accompanied by a look of gratitude so exquisitely touching as frequently to draw tears from the most insensible spectators.

" It was not possible to be mistaken with regard to the sincerity of these poor people; every thing they did shewed that they were deeply affected with the kindness they had received; and the proof that their hearts were really softened was displayed, not only in their unaffected expressions of gratitude, but also in the effusions of their affectionate regard for those who were dear to them. In short, never did I witness scenes so affecting as those which passed between some of these poor persons and their children.

" It has been mentioned that *the children were separated from the grown persons.* This was the case, however, only at first. As soon as order was thoroughly established in every part of the house, and the poor people had acquired a certain degree of address in their work, so as to take pleasure in it, many of them having expressed an earnest desire to have their children near them, permission was granted for that purpose; and the spinning-halls, by degrees, were filled with the most interesting little groups of industrious families, who vied with each other in diligence and address, and who displayed a scene at once the most busy and the most cheerful that can be imagined.

" An industrious family," observes the Count, " is ever a pleasing object; but there was something peculiarly interesting and affecting in the groups of these poor people. Whether it was that those who contemplated them compared their present situation with the state of misery and wretchedness from which they had been taken, or whether it was the joy and exultation which were expressed in the countenances of the parents themselves in contemplating their children all busily employed about them, or the air of self-satisfaction which these little urchins put on at the consciousness of their own dexterity, while they pursued their work with redoubled diligence upon being observed, which rendered the scene so singularly interesting, I know not; but certain it is, that few strangers who visited the establishment came out of these halls without being much affected."

THE writer of this work recommends to all who are engaged in the superintendance and management of the poor in this country the attentive perusal of the preceding sketch. It is particularly valuable to such persons; as being minutely descriptive of the feeling recently and very successfully adopted in Bavaria towards a most abject class of our fellow-beings, namely, the mendicant paupers of that country. It affords also a very compendious out-line of the *nature* of those *cares* which every government should manifest towards its own labouring poor. If these latter consti-tute the active strength of a community; if they may be compared to the *hands* and *feet* of a human body, the labours of which cannot be dispensed with; then are the labours of the *head*, to *plan* and *stimulate* and *reward*, equally indispensable. When, however, the real interests of this class of people are no longer con-sidered; when their comforts are abridged, and that spirit of inde-pendence which produced their best efforts is gone; the most well-grounded apprehensions may be entertained for the peace and the welfare of such a country. It may be repeated, too, that the facul-ties of man are not only by nature *active*, but have a stronger tendency to *evil* than to *good*, unless they are most carefully directed to some useful and appropriate employment; and that the *employment* of the poor is, therefore, a genuine kindness, and more truly beneficial to them than *gratuitous alms*. Those who have visited richly endowed almshouses will be at no loss con-cerning the application of this last remark. It is an undoubted fact, that though the inmates of these houses are amply provided for, and their every want liberally anticipated, yet they are gene-rally dissatisfied and listless: a secret *ennui* prevails among them, for want of useful and necessary employment. It is evident, then, that if occupation were *not* to produce pecuniary profit (which is its legitimate aim), yet it soothes the mind, enlivens the spirits, promotes health, and is the best means of diminishing the many troubles to which poverty is ever subject: for which reason, he who enables a poor man to obtain *moderate* and *healthy* employ-ment does him a far greater kindness than in giving him a pension for life for doing nothing. " In all labour there is profit," saith the Wise Man. But idleness is the source of all mischief, and the parent of every crime.

On Machinery,

AS APPLIED TO MANUFACTURES.

IN our endeavours to advocate the general employment of the poor, it is proper that we should take some notice of the extensive use which has been made of the mechanical powers, in the produce of manufactured articles. The grand invention of the steam-engine is, without doubt, a signal triumph of the intellectual, over the bodily faculties of man. And we look with admiration on a piece of machinery, which, by the intervention of several thousands of wheels, impelled by the power of steam or water, will produce an almost endless variety of movements. But our researches, even of a scientific nature, may be too ardently pursued, and carry us beyond the limits assigned to them by our infinitely wise Creator. It is when the energy of individuals is found to be detrimental to the welfare of society, that it should excite mistrust and alarm; and it is at such a period, too, that it becomes the duty of legislators, and persons possessed of influence and sound philanthropy, to interfere with, and restrain its further progress.

The prevailing opinions on the subject of Machinery, as applied to Manufactures, are at present contradictory and much encumbered with party feeling. While some persons ascribe its rapid advance to the late wonderful extension of science and knowledge in general others view it as the offspring of desolation, produced by the exterminating influence of *war*. The humane observer, however, sees and knows that its course has been marked by a painful excess of suffering amongst the labouring classes of the community. The sources of regular industry and comfortable support seem to be fast closing on those unfortunate people, who are, perhaps, of all classes, the least capable of changing the nature of their occupations, and of accommodating themselves to the variations which either science or fashion is always too ready to impose on human industry. We cannot be mistaken in those multiplied statements of facts that have been incessantly pouring forth of late years from our manufacturing districts. Though some cases of exaggeration may occur, yet the *general voice* must be the *voice of truth*. We are told that, in those districts, large numbers of the lesser tradesmen and manufacturers have been ruined since the adoption of machinery; that men of private merit, who, at the commencement of the struggle, combated the distresses of the times, and supported their families under those circumstances, in respectability and comfort, are now reduced to the condition of journeymen, or day labourers; and occasionally accept relief from the parish! We will not attempt to describe the probable sufferings of these people before they could have brought themselves to claim relief from a source so humiliating and degrading! But this is not all. The formerly successful owner of a manufacturing steam-engine—he who, by expending a large proportion of his capital on machinery, did, at the first setting-out, obtain a proportionably extensive share of profit—is now reduced, by an increase of competing capital, to the lowest ratio of fair advantage; while the arts of the needy adventurer who undersells him at the expense of principle, the depressed market to which he carries his goods, and the progressive decay of his machinery, all conspire to threaten him with eventual failure and disgrace. Should it be objected against this man, that he had formely cherished schemes of self-aggrandizement and exclusive wealth, at the expense of the labouring classes, and of many tens and hundreds of industrious individuals around him, still this is no consolation to the lover and promoter of virtue and happiness among mankind. He feels assured that there must be something fundamentally wrong in a state of things that is productive of evils such as these. It affords considerable satisfaction, too, while we are taking this view of the subject, to know that there are, amongst the master-manufacturers themselves, writers who afford us strong evidence of the truth and correctness of these general propositions. ROBERT OWEN, of New-Lanark, a proprietor of one of the largest Cotton Factories in Great-Britain, and a man entitled to respect as an experienced manufacturer and a philanthropist, whatever peculiarities may exist with regard to his religious opinions, makes the following striking observations:

" Hitherto legislators have appeared to regard manufactures only in one point of view—as a source of national wealth. The other mighty consequences which proceed from extended manufactures, *when left to their natural progress,* have never yet engaged the attention of the legislature. Yet the political and moral effects to which we allude, well deserve to occupy the best faculties of the greatest and wisest statesmen.

" The general diffusion of manufactures throughout a country generates a new character in its inhabitants; and as this character is formed upon a principle quite unfavourable to individual or general happiness, it will produce the most lamentable and permanent evils, unless its tendency be counteracted by legislative interference and direction.

" The manufacturing system has already so far extended its influence over the British empire, as to effect an essential change in the general mass of the people. This alteration is still in rapid progress: and ere long, the comparatively happy simplicity of the agricultural peasant will be wholly lost amongst us; it is even now scarcely anywhere to be found, without a mixture of those habits which are the offspring of trade, manufactures, and commerce.

" The industry of the lower orders, from whose labour wealth is drawn, has been carried, by new competitors striving against those of longer standing, *to a point of oppression;* reducing them, by successive changes, as the spirit of competition increased, and the ease of acquiring wealth diminished, to a state more wretched than can be imagined by those who have not attentively observed the changes as they have gradually occurred. In consequence, they are at present in a situation infinitely more degraded and miserable than they were before the introduction of these manufactories, upon the success of which their bare subsistence now depends."

The following description, also, which is drawn from life by the same writer, must excite feelings of deep commiseration in the breast of every reader:

",In the manufacturing districts, it is common for parents to send children of both sexes, at seven or eight years of age, in winter as well as summer, at six o'clock in the morning, sometimes of course in the dark, and occasionally amidst frost and snow, to enter the manufactories, which are often heated to a high temperature, and contain an atmosphere far from being the most favourable to human life; and in which all those employed in them very frequently continue until twelve o'clock at noon, when an hour is allowed for dinner; after which they return, and remain, in a majority of cases, till eight o'clock at night.

" The children now find they must labour incessantly for their bare subsistence. They have not been accustomed to innocent, healthy, and rational amusements; they are not permitted the requisite time, if they had previously been accustomed to enjoy them. They know not what relaxation means, except by the actual cessation from labour. They are surrounded by others similarly circumstanced with themselves; and thus passing on from childhood to youth, they become gradually initiated, the young men in particular, but often the young females also, in the seductive pleasures of the alehouse and inebriation; for which their daily hard labour, want of better habits, and the general vacuity of their minds, tend to prepare them.

" Such a system of training cannot be expected to produce any other than a population weak in bodily and mental faculties, and with habits generally destructive of their own comforts, of the well-being of those around them, and strongly calculated to subdue all the social affections. Man so circumstanced, sees all around him hurrying forward at a mail-coach speed, to acquire individual wealth; regardless of him, his comforts, his wants, or even his sufferings, except by way of *degrading parish charity*, fitted only to steel the heart of man against his fellows, or to form the tyrant and the slave. To-day he labours for one master, to-morrow for a second, then for a third, and a fourth, until all ties between employers and employed are frittered down to the consideration of what immediate gain each can derive from the other. The employer regards the employed as mere instruments of gain; while these acquire a gross ferocity of character, which, if legislative measures shall not be judiciously devised to prevent its increase, and ameliorate the condition of this class, will sooner or later plunge the country into a formidable and perhaps inextricable state of danger."[*]

If this be a faithful picture of the present condition of the labouring classes in our manufacturing towns, we may safely assert that the proprietor of a woollen or cotton factory, conducted on these principles, is almost as great an enemy to the health, morals, and happiness of mankind as the wholesale dealer in slaves ever was, or can be! The *minds* of negro-slaves have never been sold with their bodies; but here is the most complete *mental* as well as *bodily* subjugation, produced by the sordid unfeeling use of a single piece of mechanim! Well may the moralist shudder in the midst of his conveniencies, if such be the price which society pays for their prodnction!

It may here occur to some close thinker, that this condition to which his fellow-creatures are reduced, if it be slavery, is at least *voluntary;* and he will perhaps think it right to look upon the *freedom of the human will* as a possession that balances all the excesses of human misery. But the advocate of humanity, the friend of all the sweet offices of philanthropy, does not entertain so cold and calculating a view of the subject. It is obvious to him, that voluntary slavery (if so paradoxical an expression may be used to designate this monstrous production of society), in a thickly populated country, is the most insupportable of all slavery. The negro in the West-India plantations, who has his hours of labour and of rest *allotted for him,* who possesses his hut and his little garden, *even at the pleasure of his master,* is superlatively happy when his privileges are balanced with those of the labouring manufacturer in England. It is, however, but just to observe, that there are honourable exceptions amongst the proprietors of these immense factories, though the necessary assemblage of so vast a multitude of both sexes must render it very difficult to avoid demoralizing consequences.

---

[*] Owen's " *Observations on the Effect of the Manufacturing System.*"

At New-Lanark the utmost care is taken of the morals of the children; and it generally is so managed, that the boys and girls work in different apartments. Besides which, the strictest attention is paid to their mental instruction in the Sunday Schools, which have long been established on the premises by the humane proprietor of this extensive factory.—The same care is taken of the morals and comfort of the poor employed by Fox and Sons, in their extensive woollen-factory near Wellington.

We wish the like conscientious regard to the welfare of the poor was general throughout this kingdom. If such were the case, if masters considered themselves more often as the *fathers* of the great *families* over which they preside, the gross immorality which we have now to deplore would not, probably, prevail, as it unhappily does at present. Still, where a promiscuous intercourse takes place between the sexes, from their childhood, the uniform consequence must be, that habits of debauchery become general at a very early age.

Under the influence of this unhappy depravity in large factories, can we wonder that the morals as well as the physical strength of their population should degenerate to the lowest guage of wretchedness? Their meagre, pallid countenances, and their vacant, untutored minds, evince the utmost human degradation.—As wives or mothers, the wretched females seem almost wholly incapable of performing any other duties than the monotonous employments which entitle them to their daily or weekly pittance.

Previously to the commencement of the late war with France, somewhat more than 30 years since, the writer of these pages was concerned in a considerable woollen-manufacture in Hampshire, which employed upwards of 2,000 spinners. In the same district there were other manufacturers who employed perhaps nearly an equal number of hands. These spinners received 2s. 3s. 4s. and even 5s. per pound for the wool they spun. Some of the yarn was of the finest texture, and was used in making poplins, bombazeens, and other goods of the most curious fabric.

The wages which these industrious females received, enabled them not only to purchase a sufficiency of food, but they could generally spare a fourth part of their earnings for the purchase of clothing, which was supplied by the master manufacturers. But now, alas! this source of comparative wealth to numerous families of industrious cottagers is almost entirely absorbed, if not annihilated, by the introduction of *spinning-jennies*. And the daily pursuits of Agriculture among these people are no longer followed by the cheerful evening task of fine spinning, accompanied with those peaceful and satisfied feelings to which moderate occupation never fails to give birth. If this be a specimen of the actual effects produced by machinery, of this kind, throughout the kingdom (and there is no doubt that it is so for the most part), how injurious to the morals and comfort of thousands and tens of thousands of the labouring poor such a transition must have proved, let the sordid votaries of gain and the promoters of the war-spirit decide!

The following extract is from R. OWEN's "Letter on his Plan for abolishing Pauperism:"

"When peace returned, it found Great-Britain in possession of a new power in constant action, which, it may be safely stated, exceeded the exertions of *one hundred millions* of the most industrious human beings, in the full strength of manhood.

" Thus our country possessed, at the conclusion of the war, a productive power, which operated to the same effect as if her population had been actually increased *fifteen* or *twenty fold:* and this had been chiefly created within the preceding twenty-five years. The rapid progress made by Great-Britain during the war, in wealth and political influence, can therefore no longer astonish; the cause was quite adequate to the effect.

"Now, however, new circumstances have arisen. The war demand for productions of labour having ceased, markets could no longer be found for them; and the revenues of the world were inadequate to purchase that which a power so enormous in its effects did produce. A diminished demand consequently followed. When, therefore, it became necessary to contract the sources of supply, it soon proved that mechanical power was much cheaper than human labour: the former, in consequence, was continued at work, while the latter was superseded; and human labour may now be obtained at a price far less than is absolutely necessary for the subsistence of the individual in ordinary comfort.

" Human labour, hitherto the great source of wealth in nations, being thus diminished in value, at the rate of not less than *two or three millions* sterling per week in Great-Britain alone, that sum, or whatever more or less it may be, has consequently been withdrawn from the circulation of the country, and has necessarily been the means by which the farmer, tradesman, manufacturer, and merchant, have been so greatly impoverished.

" A little reflection will shew, that as the working classes have now no adequate means of contending with mechanical power, one of the three following results must therefore ensue :

" 1st. The use of mechanism must be greatly diminished; or,

" 2d. Millions of human beings must be starved, if its existence be permitted to its present extent; or,

" 3d. Advantageous occupation must be found for the poor and unemployed working classes, to whose labour mechanism must be rendered subservient, instead of being applied, as at present, to supersede it.

"But, under the existing commercial system, mechanical power cannot in one country be discontinued, and in others remain in action, without ruin to that country in which it is discontinued. No one nation, therefore, will discontinue it; and although such an act were possible, it would be a sure sign of barbarism in those who should make the attempt. *It would, however, be a far more evident sign of barbarism, and an act of gross tyranny, were any government to permit mechanical power to starve millions of human beings.* The thought will not admit of one moment's contemplation. It would inevitably create unheard of misery to all ranks. The last result, therefore, alone deserves to be considered; which is, that 'advantageous occupation must be found for the unemployed working classes, to whose labour mechanism must be rendered *subservient*, instead of being applied, as at present, to supersede it.'

"To conduct a change so important, and of such vital necessity to our well-being, demands a comprehensive view, and an accurate knowledge, of the real state of society. The measure should be well considered with respect to its present bearings and connexions, and its consequences traced by minds uninfluenced by prejudice of party or of class.

"The circumstances of the times render a change in our internal policy respecting the poor and working classes absolutely necessary; and the first question to be decided by every man of all ranks is—Shall the alteration be made under the guidance of moderation and wisdom, foreseeing, and gradually preparing each step, one regularly after another, thereby preventing a single premature advance? or shall the change be effected by ignorance and prejudice, under the baleful influence of the angry and violent passions? Should these prevail, then will the truly disinterested, those whose ardent wish is to ameliorate the condition of mankind, withdraw from the contest, and society be involved in confusion. But surely the experience of past ages, and particularly of the last twenty-five years, will have taught men wisdom, and prepared the minds of all for a calm and dispassionate inquiry, how the evils which at present afflict society can be best remedied.*

GILBERT ROTTON, of Frome, a gentleman whose long residence in that large manufacturing town, together with his experience in the clothing business, fully qualify him to judge of this interesting subject, writes thus:

"Machinery may be beneficial to a nation when engaged in long and destructive wars, or when from any other cause the population is not equal to the demand for labour. Such was the case with this country during the late wars.

"England, from a coincidence of circumstances which are not likely to occur again, became the *manufactory*, if I may be allowed the expression, for the whole world. The demand for labour increased in a rapid and to a wonderful extent, and the labourers decreased almost as rapidly, being drained off to supply our army and navy. In this crisis machinery was not merely beneficial, it was our salvation: *we could not possibly have done without it*. But our situation is now completely reversed. We are no longer the emporium of Europe: our labourers no longer find employ in our army and navy. Machinery still however supplies the place of those hands which we wanted during the war; and the consequence is, that the labourer is excluded from labour, and must perish for want, or be maintained in idleness by those who are able to contribute to his support.

"It is clear, from the great increase of the poor-rates and the thousands of starving poor, that there are now sufficient labourers to supply all the demand we should have for labour, if machinery were not used; and that at as reasonable a rate to the nation, or nearly so, as it can be supplied by machinery.

"Mr. Malthus says, the use of machinery extends the demand for the commodity, by enabling the manufacturer to bring his goods to market cheaper. This may be true, if applied to a country either where the commodity has not been previously manufactured, or where the labourers have full employ in other pursuits, or where the demand for labour exceeds the supply. But in a country where there is a redundancy of workmen, where the demand for the commodity decreases, or where the manufactory has been previously established and carried on by manual labour, machinery is and must be highly injurious.

"In this country, machinery, at present, instead of extending, decreases the demand for the commodity, because it throws the working classes, who, as a body, are the greatest purchasers, out of the market. By the use of machinery thousands are not only rendered unable to obtain a surplus of wages beyond what will supply them with food, but are prevented from obtaining any wages, except the wages of idleness—*parish pay*. I maintain, therefore, that the use of machinery, in the present state of this country, is highly injurious; and it is the sole cause of the want of employ of by far the greater proportion of the working classes.

"It is also asserted by the advocates of machinery, that by its use we can render the manufactured articles cheaper, and that without it we could not enter into competition with foreigners: both these positions I deny. Suppose a manufacturer to employ 100 men, who together earn 50*l.* a-week for their wages. A machine is invented, which requires, we will say, 5 men only, to do the work of 100: he turns off 95 men, who for want of employ are obliged to apply to the parish for a maintenance. Now it is true, the manufacturer makes his goods cheaper, because he saves about

47*l.* weekly in wages, and individually he is benefitted; and why? Because he manufactures at the expense of the other inhabitants of the parish, who have now to maintain his 95 workmen and their families, at a charge little, if any thing, short of what the manufacturer saves by using the machine. This, in my opinion, is the proper way of viewing the subject; not as it affects the individual, but as it affects the nation. And taken in this point of view, the parish rates will prove that *it costs the nation much more at present to manufacture goods by machinery than it would by manual labour.* We are enabled to undersell foreigners merely by the aid of a *parish tax,* which is tantamount to a bounty to the manufacturer on all the goods sold. But the fact is, the manufacturer saves very little by his machinery; for after he calculates a fair yearly proportion of the prime cost of the machine, the wear and tear, the rent for additional buildings, and other *et cetera,* he will find the weekly expenditure to equal, if not exceed, the wages previously paid.

" Again: as it affects the nation. We are not to suppose its bad effects extend only to the tax levied on the parish, or to the exclusion of the 95 men and their families from the market: it obliges those who have to support the unemployed to retrench their expenditure in every possible way. Look at our shops, and we shall soon be convinced how extensively mischievous are its effects in a country abounding with an unemployed population. How, therefore, can it be said that we are enabled to manufacture cheaper by the aid of machinery, or that it is beneficial to the nation?

" Machinery costs us 5 or 6 millions a-year at least in poor-rates; it decreases the demand, not only for the manufactured articles, but for articles of foreign growth and agricultural produce; it reduces two-thirds of our population to extreme indigence and idleness; it is destructive in a high degree of every moral quality; it renders ineffectual every effort to ameliorate the condition of the poor; and it will, sooner or later, upset the Government or destroy the Constitution. No nation can long continue internally peaceable or prosperous, when the great majority of the population are reduced to beggary and idleness."

GILBERT ROTTON'S SECOND LETTER
ON MACHINERY.

" DEAR SIR,—I have already observed, that Mr. Malthus was mistaken in supposing that the use of machinery throws capital out of employ; but, before I attempt to controvert his opinion on this point, I cannot refrain from making a few observations on the effects which machinery produces on the *morals* of the working-classes. I have said it is destructive, in a high degree, of every *moral* quality; and I appeal to every observing and impartial person, residing in, or near manufacturing places, whether my assertion be not strictly correct. The use of machinery obliges the manufacturer to collect a great number of his workpeople *under one roof*; and there we may observe, working together indiscriminately, men and women, boys and girls. Here one or two bad characters suffice to corrupt the whole mass; and they actually do so, with few exceptions. The infant eye and ear are constantly accustomed to all kinds of ribaldry, blasphemy, and obscenity. I know, that, in this town, every exertion possible is made to counteract the mischief, by the individual efforts of the employers, and by the establishment of Sunday-schools, &c.; but what can avail against such an education—such an overwhelming moral contagion? It may be conjectured, that the consequences *might* have been the same, even though machinery had not been introduced; and that these are only the natural effects of an indiscriminate mixture of the sexes, in a manufactory, either with or without machinery. But, in reply, 1 say, had not machinery been introduced, there would have been no necessity for such a collection of both sexes under one roof. I do not mean, however, to be understood that this evil admits not of a remedy, even though the use of machinery should be extended; on the contrary, I think it may be easily checked, by having separate buildings, or separate rooms for the different sexes; and placing in each room a person of good moral habits, who should report to the master any improper behaviour. Care also should be taken to make the females retire to their homes, when the hours of employ are over. Previously to the introduction of machinery, the labouring poor, for many miles round a manufacturing town, were supplied at their own homes with the raw material, to forward it in some one or other of its stages; namely, carding, spinning, &c. I have been informed by persons now living, that 40 years ago, wool was distributed to the cottagers, at the distance of 40 or 50 miles round Frome, for the purpose of being spun, &c. This must have been, at times, I allow, very harassing and inconvenient to the manufacturer; but in every other point of view, it was surely beneficial: it carried employment and comfort to the poor of all the surrounding parishes; the children were brought up under the eye of their parents, in habits of industry, and being distant from the alehouse, and other scenes of vice, moral contamination was thus prevented, or speedily checked.

" I have not painted the immoral tendency of a factory-education in too high colours, but the reverse. I could state facts that are known to many persons, and describe scenes that I have beheld, and relate speeches that I have heard from boys and girls, *not nine years old*, that would make humanity shudder.

" Mr. Malthus supposes a case of a number of capitalists employing 20,000*l.* each in a manufacture; and that machines were introduced, which, by the saving of labour, would enable them to carry on the same trade, with capitals of 10,000*l.* each. In which case, a certain proportion of the ten thousand pounds, and of the men employed, would be disengaged, and ready for some other employ. And the conclusion drawn, is, that the money, thus set free, would be used in the purchase of fresh commodities. Supposing this to be correct, Mr. Malthus himself proceeds to state sufficient, to convince us that the introduction of machinery can be but a questionable benefit. The *fact* is, however, otherwise; for the introduction of machinery does not, in general, disengage capital, to be re-employed in some other beneficial way. It enables a manufacturer to discharge a great many work-people, and to withdraw so much of his capital as is employed in the payment of *their wages;* but so far from this portion of his capital being set at liberty, it is immediately wanted, together with *much more,* for the purpose of purchasing machinery, erecting buildings, and paying millwrights' work, &c. And I suppose it will not be denied, that whatever is thus expended, becomes capital. To this must be added the necessary wear and tear, the constant repair and replacing of machinery and buildings; the loss sustained when trade is dull, and the manufacturer cannot fully employ his buildings and machinery, which then become a dead and unprofitable capital; and then, I think I may assert, without the fear of contradiction, that so far from machinery *disengaging,* it demands, if any thing, *a larger capital* to carry on the same extent of trade to advantage. *With* the aid of machinery, however, and a brisk trade, a manufacturer may be enabled to make *greater profits,* and thereby create an *additional* capital; but that is foreign to the point in question. If it was actually the case that machinery disengages capital as well as men, and that such capital could be immediately engaged in some other productive way, so as to employ the men thrown out of work, little injury would be done. But, as it appears clear, that machinery throws *men, and not capital,* out of employ, the mischief is great, and must increase with the increasing use of machinery.

"Another assertion of Mr. Malthus I think equally incorrect. It is, that Machinery, by saving labour, and enabling us to bring goods to market cheaper, extends the demand for the commodity, *and that more hands, instead of fewer, are thus required;* and he instances the cotton trade, as employing more hands, and being of infinitely more value *now*, than it was 30 years since. But surely, Mr. Malthus needs not to be informed, that, 30 years ago, the cotton trade was but in its infancy, in this country; and that the state of the world, during the last 30 years, has tended to the extension of that branch of our trade, as well as every other. England, during nearly the whole of that time, had supplied all other nations! And, besides, the cotton trade has extended itself, to the *ruin of other manufactures* in this country, particularly the Salisbury and Devonshire woollens, which used, formerly, to constitute the clothing of nearly all the females of the lower ranks in society. The success of the cotton trade is, therefore, no proof of the truth of Mr. Malthus's assertion. He cannot certainly mean to assert, that the introduction of a machine, which does the labour of 50 persons, can be the means of increasing the demand for labour. Can the use of a threshing-machine, for instance, which will, *in a few days,* perform what would have employed 8 or 10 men *all the winter,*—or that a of gig-mill, which, with its proper proportion of shearing-frames, will enable the clothier to turn off 30 men,—*increase* the demand for labourers? Our woollen trade increased, during the war, nearly as much, in proportion, as the cotton trade; and it is now much more extensive, than it was previously to the introduction of machinery; *but it does not employ one-half of the number of workpeople which it did formerly.* Our trade must wonderfully increase indeed, before it can counteract, or even balance, the effects of machinery, with its consequent abridgment of human labour: such an increase of trade, England can certainly never expect to see again!

"Though it would seem, from the parts of Mr. Malthus's work which I have before commented on, that he is an advocate for the use of machinery, he is so under contingencies only; and which, in fact, amount to this, that the demand for the commodity keeps pace with its increased production by machinery. But this is no longer the case with us; nor have we any reason to expect that it will ever again be so. Indeed, had the war continued, the demand for our goods would not have increased; for so great had been the production, from the increased use of machinery, during the last 3 or 4 years of the war, that the markets were almost glutted, and the manufacturers began, most seriously, to feel the ill consequences. Machinery must have this effect, sooner or later, even under the most favourable circumstances. And in a state of peace, restricted in our markets, and with almost the certainty of a continually decreasing demand, the manufacturer must carry on his business with dread and uncertainty; because he will have a constantly fluctuating market, and the more than probable chance, that great part of what he manufactures will remain on hand for a considerable time. Such, now, is the facility of production, from the quantity of machinery in this country, both in the cotton and woollen trade, that sufficient goods of both kinds could be made, in one year, to supply all the demands that can possibly arise in three. I think I shall not go beyond the truth, when I assert, that if all the machinery in the clothing trade were to be fully employed for three months, more cloth would be made than could be used in Great-Britain, and all its dependencies, for two years!!

"Another disadvantage arising to the fair trader from the introduction of machinery, is the facility it gives to dishonest and pennyless persons, engaging in trade. It is a fact, that a person may now commence clothier, without having any capital; or rather that he can, without having any capital himself, get cloth manufactured for him. He can buy all the materials, at a credit of 6, 8, or 12 months; he can have the wool dyed, spun, wove, milled, dressed, and sent home to him in cloth, fit for the market, *all on credit*. Many persons engage in the trade on this plan; and the consequence is, that in order to meet their payments, a quantity of cloth is constantly thrown into the market, at a price generally *under prime cost*.

"The capitalist stands no chance of fair competition with such men. *He* has something to lose, *they* have nothing; and they are reckless of the event. I refer not to industrious small tradesmen, who commence with little capital, but whom we see proceeding by gradual steps, and seldom going beyond their means.

"Before the introduction of machinery, a man could not have engaged in the business, without a capital. He might, it is true have obtained credit for his wool, and for dying, but he must have found ready money for all the rest.

"It has been said by some that machinery is beneficial to the country, because the facility of production, and the consequent greater quantity produced, tend to enrich the country. This, however, I deny, unless the greater quantity be of greater value than the smaller; and to be so, the demand for the greater quantity must be in proportion; and it must yield a proportionate price. I do not mean to contend, that the nation is benefitted by great individual profits, arising from the manufacturers; but I do mean to contend, that as national wealth is made up of individual wealth, it is nonsense to assert that the nation is enriched by the ruin of a body of manufacturers.

"Every commodity should yield something more than the prime cost of its production: if it does not, it cannot add to the wealth, either of the producer or of the nation.

"Having endeavoured to point out the evils arising from the use of machinery, it may be expected of me, now, to say how I think those evils may be remedied. On this subject, however, I cannot at present enter; for reasons that must be obvious to every thinking mind. I shall only observe, that whatever is done, must be done *gradually;* and that the manufacturers themselves may do considerable immediate good, by discontinuing the use of those machines, which only tend to throw work-people out of employ, without improving the commodity manufactured, or diminishing its price. I would instance, in the clothing-trade, the gig-mills and shearing-frames; from the use of which, I think the clothiers have been great sufferers, and the cloth has been materially injured. However, perhaps no good can be expected, without the interference of the Legislature. THAT SOMETHING SHOULD BE DONE, AND THAT SPEEDILY, I THINK EVERY HUMANE MIND, EVERY WELLWISHER TO HIS COUNTRY WILL ALLOW.

"You are at liberty, my dear Sir, to make use of either of my letters, in your intended work, in any way that you may think proper; and with best wishes for the success of your benevolent design, I remain, Yours, &c.

Frome, 28th *Nov.* 1820. GILBERT ROTTON."

On Agricultural Employments.

THE culture of the earth was doubtless the first employment of mankind, at the earliest period of the world, ; and it is not only necessary, but has been ever esteemed honourable, and conducive to virtue and happiness. The chief subsistence of mankind, in civilized society being derived from the earth, the cultivators of it have, in all ages, been considered as justly entitled to public encouragement, from motives of common interest.

In this country, however, it is generally allowed, that the state of agriculture was never more depressed than it is at present. The farmers in many places are unable to pay their rent and taxes; whilst their labourers, with the utmost industry and toil, cannot earn sufficient wages to procure the bare necessaries of life, without submitting to the unmerited degradation of seeking relief from the parish.

In the agricultural districts, we understand, it is a common practice for labourers in husbandry to receive from their employers the low wages of 5s. or 6s. per week; and as this is insufficient for their support and that of their families, the remainder of the allowance required barely to support a miserable existence, is supplied from the poor-rates of the parish. And this scanty pittance is not unfrequently doled out to deserving men, accompanied with terms of upbraiding, by parish officers.

To such conduct, the complaint of the Apostle appears to be not inapplicable: " Behold, the hire of the labourers, which have reaped down your fields, which is of you kept back by fraud, crieth: and the cries of them which have reaped are entered into the ears of the LORD of sabaoth." James v. 4.

This practice of paying workmen part of what they are justly entitled to, in compensation for their labour, by way of boon from the parish, appears utterly contrary to every principle of moral justice and wise policy, and must tend to destroy every feeling of manly exertion, and desire of self-support, in men so undeservedly treated.

Whether this ruinous system of policy may be the offspring of *war*, and its inseparable attendant *excessive taxation*, we shall not take upon us to determine; the fact, however, of scanty employment, insufficient wages, and general distress among the labourers in agriculture, is, we believe, too well known to admit of a doubt.

In any other country excepting our own, we should be inclined to suspect, either that the laws were defective, or that those who administered them neglected to do their duty. And yet it is certainly true, that, in England, the industrious husbandman, who toils hard during the heat of summer and the cold of winter, in raising food for the rich, who do *not* labour, as well as for the poor who *do*, with all his toil and privations, does not receive wages sufficient to procure him the common necessaries of life. Can this be just? We ask, Can it be right?

Next to the low rate of wages which the husbandman receives, the recent inventions in machinery, (we cannot call them *improvements*) used in farming business, have proved very injurious to poor labourers. Formerly, old men, whose limbs were grown stiff by hard labour in their youth, found a comfortable asylum from the wet and cold of winter, in threshing out their master's corn until the return of the spring, when they could again work out of doors. Now, on most large farms, threshing machines are introduced, which supersede the formerly comfortable employment of these superannuated labourers. It appears that a threshing-machine, with the use of two horses, and one man, with two women or boys, can perform the work of twelve men in an ordinary way; consequently eleven men must be thrown out of employ by this machine; and, most likely be driven to the workhouse if they are old, or pine in sorrow in their own comfortless hovels, probably with little food and less firing.

The advanced state of science has, besides, introduced various other machines into farms; all of which tend, more or less, to abridge human labour, and to deprive the poor of their accustomed employments.

Can we wonder that these things excite discontent among the poor, whose labour is their only natural inheritance? It would rather be a subject of wonder if the labourer *could* submit to be deprived of his just and reasonable support, without murmuring. It is cruel, it is unjust to make an industrious man, who is willing and able to support himself by his labour, a *pauper*, in the most degrading sense of the word.

The condition of labourers in agriculture, and especially of that class of men properly designated " peasants," appears to have been gradually on the decline amongst us for at least half a century. It became a pretty general practice about that time to convert many of the small farms into larger ones; which practice, however convenient it might have been to Landholders, in enabling them to receive their rents from one tenant instead of half a dozen, certainly proved injurious to the general interests of society. The small farmers, if they were not possessed of sufficient capital to undertake an enlarged farm, were then necessarily obliged to become servants or day-labourers, probably on the same land which they had before cultivated as masters.

Previously to the period alluded to, many a small farmer had lived respectably, and brought up his family in habits of industry and virtue, on farms, the rental of which, in those days, was perhaps, not more than from 10*l.* to 30*l.* per annum; and it is believed that the land thus managed, yielded as much to the public, as it has since done on the monopolizing system.

It is true, these little farmers, and their wives and children, all laboured hard, but they did it cheerfully, from the reflection that they worked for themselves, and not for a master. Their crops, both of hay and corn, were generally got together in as good condition as on larger farms, if not better, especially if the weather was unfavourable; because every hand that could be useful, whether young or old, male or female, was put in requisition on such occasions. Besides, the assistance of most of the neighbouring villagers was gratuitously afforded to these little farmers, if required. Of the corn scattered on the ground, nothing was wasted; as a larger stock of pigs and poultry, in proportion to the size of the farms, was then kept than it would be possible to keep on farms more widely extended from the farm-house. Our markets were, of course, supplied with greater abundance of small articles, such as eggs, butter, poultry, and pork, than they have since been.

The females too, were generally as usefully and industriously occupied as the males; that portion of their time which was not taken up in the dairy, and looking after the poultry and pigs, or in attending to the necessary concerns of the family, was, in many cases, occupied in carding or spinning wool, knitting, sewing, mending or making garments for themselves, and the males of the family. However the wives and daughters of great farmers in the present day, may look upon these employments with disdain, they were such as princesses, and other females of the first distinction, in ancient times, considered it a part of their duty to be engaged in.

It was also from our peasants, or little farmers, that the most valuable female servants were wont to be obtained,—young women, whose early habits had sprung from industry, morality, and virtue, carefully inculcated, both in the way of precept and example by their parents. Since this hardy and useful class of people is become almost extinct in England, we need not wonder at the complaint universally heard amongst us, concerning " *bad servants.*"

The practice of throwing small farms into large ones, has produced other evils besides those already mentioned. It has had a demoralizing effect on the young and unmarried men employed on farms, who were formerly supplied with their food and lodging in the farm-houses. These men were accustomed to receive a sufficiency of plain wholesome provisions, and, after the labours of the day, to retire early to bed. But, in the present day, the wives and daughters of great farmers are of a different description of persons from the industrious females above alluded to. They have been educated at boarding-schools, where they have learnt any thing but the correct use of their mother-tongue, the command of the substantial rules of arithmetic, and those arts of economy without which no station in life, either high or low, can be well or durably maintained. Of course, the false pride they acquire, by an unsuitable education, makes them esteem it a drudgery to carry eggs, butter, or poultry to market, or to provide suitable food for a number of workmen. The latter are, consequently, obliged to get their board and lodging where they can; probably at some public-house, where their time and their money are spent alike unprofitably. Can we wonder that such men become *paupers* as soon as they get married, and have a family; and that they continue paupers as long as they live? It may also be observed here, while we are alluding to those habits in females which were formerly advantageous to the interests of virtue, morality, and the well-being of society, that, in the times we have been speaking of, the *garments* of the peasants were such as best answered the purposes of clothing: they were plain, substantial, and comfortable. No attempts to appear in flimsey finery had yet been made by this class of people. They had not learnt to *purchase* clothing at a *cheap* rate, in order to *wear* it at a *dear* one. Nor had the varieties of modern luxury obtained admittance into their dwellings. Even their food was not less remarkable for its simplicity than their apparel. Fashion may smile while we not only call in question the salubrious qualities of foreign tea as a common beverage, but even pronounce it *pernicious* to the labourer. This herb was not commonly used in farm-houses, nor amongst the poor, generally, fifty years ago; but in its stead, a cheap, nutritive, and savoury porridge, in the cooking of which those herbs which the peasant's own garden supplied, and which his own industry had contributed to raise, were alone required, It would have been well for old England, if these simple manners and frugal habits had continued to prevail among her inhabitants to this day! That the very reverse is the case, is, however, sufficiently obvious to those who have observed, and felt, and lived long enough to form a *comparison*, and to estimate the difference between these two periods of time. *Formerly* comfort and happiness were to be met with among people of every rank and station; *now* poverty and universal gloom and discontent prevail all around us. Employments have become scarce, and industry has almost lost the will and the power to act, while fair dealing and solid worth have been succeeded by dishonest speculation, pride, and false show!

ON THE EFFECTS OF LAYING SMALL FARMS INTO LARGE ONES.

AFTER the writer had penned the foregoing reflections on the late aggrandizing system of farming, he had the satisfaction to find his opinions confirmed by so respectable an authority as that of the QUARTERLY REVIEW. In the 15th vol. No. 29, p. 197 of that work, it is observed that,

"The improved system of farming has lessened the comforts of the poor. It has either deprived the cottager of those slips of land which contributed greatly to his support, or it has placed upon them an excessive or grinding rent. But, as the comforts of the cottager are diminished, his respectability and his self-respect are diminished also; and hence arises a long train of evils. The practice of farming upon a great scale has unquestionably improved the agriculture of the country; better crops are raised at less expense: but, in a national point of view, there is something more to be considered than the produce of the land, and the profit of the land-holders. The *well-being* of the people is not of less importance than the wealth of the collective body. By the system of adding "field to field," *more has been lost to the state, than has been gained to the soil: the gain may be measured by roods and perches,—but how shall the loss be calculated?* The loss is that of a link in the social chain,—of a numerous, most useful, and most respectable class, who, from the rank of small farmers, have been degraded to that of day-labourers. True it is that the ground which they occupied is more highly cultivated—the crooked hedge-rows have been thrown down—the fields are in better shape and of handsomer dimensions—the plough makes longer furrows—there is more corn and fewer weeds;—but look at the noblest produce of the earth—look at the children of the soil—look at the seeds which are sown here for immortality! Is there no deterioration there? Does the MAN stand upon the same level in society, does *he* hold the same place in his own estimation, when he works for another, as when he works for himself; when he receives his daily wages for the sweat of his brow, and there the fruit of his labour ends, as when he enjoys day by day the advantage of his former toil, and works always in hope of the recompence which is to come?

"The small farmer, or, in the language of LATIMER,* and old English feeling, the YEOMAN, had his roots in the soil,—this was the right English tree, in which our heart of oak was matured. Where he grew up, he decayed; where he first opened his eyes, there he fell asleep. He lived as his fathers lived before him, and trained up his children in the same way. The daughters of this class of men were brought up in habits of industry and frugality, in good principles, hopefully and religiously, and with a sense of character to support. Those who were not married to persons of their own rank, were placed in service; and hence the middle ranks were supplied with that race of faithful and respectable domestic servants—the diminution and gradual extinction of which is one of the evils (and not the least) that have arisen from the new system of agriculture. One of the sons succeeded, as a thing of course, to the little portion of land which his fathers had tenanted from generation to generation. If among the boys there was one of a studious turn, he became the schoolmaster of the village, or by help of endowed schools, and the wise provision which our pious ancestors made for such cases in the Universities, or perhaps the occasional bounty of a liberal patron, he was bred up for holy orders; and as in these cases natural aptitude and the strong desire alone were consulted, it was from hence that the Church received most of its ablest and most distinguished members. The sense of family pride and family character was neither less powerful nor less beneficial, in this humble rank, than it is in the noblest families, when it takes its best direction. But old tenants have been cut down with as little remorse, and as little discrimination as old timber,—and the moral scene is in consequence as lamentably injured as the landscape!

"If the small farmer did not acquire wealth, he kept his station. The land which he had tilled with the sweat of his brow, while his strength lasted, supported him when his strength was gone: his sons did the work when he could work no longer; he had his place in the chimney-corner, or the bee-hive chair; and it was the light of his own fire that shone upon his grey hairs. Compare this with the old age of the day-labourer, with parish allowance for a time, and the parish workhouse at last. He who lives by the wages of daily labour, and can only live upon those wages, without laying up store for the morrow, is spending his capital: a time must come when it will fail; in the road that he must travel, *the poor-house is his last stage on the way to the grave!* Hence it arises, as a natural result, that looking to the parish as his ultimate resource, and as that to

---

* The father of BISHOP LATIMER was a *yeoman* who lived and brought up a family reputably, kept hospitality with his neighbours, and gave alms to the poor, on a farm of less than *ten* pounds per year! Blush, grandeur; blush !

which he must come at last, the day-labourer cares not how soon he applies to it. There is neither *hope* nor *pride* to withhold him; why should he deny himself any indulgence in youth, or why make any efforts to put off for a *little while* that which is inevitable in the end? That the labouring poor feel thus, and reason thus, and act in consequence, is beyond all doubt; and if the landholders were to count up what they have gained by throwing their estates into large farms, and what they have *lost* by the increase of the POOR-RATES, of which that system has been one great cause, they would have little reason to congratulate themselves on the result."

On the animating influence of HOPE in cheering our peasantry, the reviewer thus proceeds:

" While small farms existed, the labouring husbandman might look on to one, as the reward of his industry and good character; it was for him the attainable point of hope, but it exists no longer; the step has been taken from the ladder, and when he looks upward now, there is a gap in the scale which no exertion on his part can possibly surmount. Is there no evil in this to the *state* as well as to the *individual?* When *hope* leaves the mind, *discontent enters it;* and where that evil spirit is in possession, it is not long before ' he taketh to him seven other spirits more wicked than himself!' The harrow has gone over the ground, and they who sow disaffection, sedition, and insurrection, find it ready for the baneful seed. With what success those seeds had been scattered by the apostles of anarchy, who are never weary in ill doing, recent events may prove. Possibly those events might not have occurred, certainly they could not have occurred *to the same extent,* if the ' improved system' had not destroyed the small farms—if great cultivators, like Aaron's rod, had not swallowed up the small farmers. The men who grow corn are never the men to set fire to it. A large proportion of the misled multitude who have been burning barns and corn-stacks, would have been aiding the civil power to repress these frantic outrages, if they had had their own little property to defend. Let us not deceive ourselves! Governments are safe in proportion as the great body of the people are contented; and men cannot be contented when they work with the prospect of want and pauperism before their eyes, as that which must be their destiny at last. *If you would secure the state from within as well as from without,* YOU MUST BETTER THE CONDITION OF THE POOR!!!"

EFFECTS OF A LIBERAL POLICY TOWARDS SMALL FARMERS AND INDUSTRIOUS LABOURERS.

IT is a mark of wisdom, as well as benevolence, in those who fill the higher stations in Society, to afford encouragement to industrious and deserving persons, who, if they had opportunities of exerting their faculties in a way for which nature has qualified them, would, it is very probable, readily give proof of superior merit. Well-directed kindness to individuals of this description, is seldom thrown away; but has often proved like seed sown on *good* ground, which generally repays the labour of the husbandman. Such assistance judiciously afforded, not only raises deserving persons in their own estimation, and that of their neighbours, but stimulates them to higher degrees of usefulness in society. If, therefore, landholders, and others possessing the means, were disposed judiciously to select objects amongst their dependents and industrious neighbours, and to hold out due encouragement to the most deserving, numerous families might be raised to a state of comfort and respectability, that are now pining in indigence and despair.

" Many are the advantages (says Sir THOS. BERNARD) which a poor man may attain by perseverance and well-directed industry; *but there must be* HOPE *to aid.* Hope is the leaven, without which the mind becomes inert, and tends only to corruption. As well might we look for the kindly fruits of the earth, without sunshine in its season, as for any product from the people, *without* HOPE."

The Reports of the " Society for bettering the Condition of the Poor," furnish a variety of striking examples in support of this interesting position, from which the following are selected as the most appropriate :

" In the year 1779, a tenant of JOHN WAY, Esq;* of Hasketon, in Suffolk, died, leaving a widow and fourteen children, the eldest of whom was a girl under fourteen years of age. He had rented fourteen acres of pasture land, on which he kept two cows, which, with a very little furniture and clothing, were all the property he left.

" The parish of Hasketon is within the district of one of the incorporated Houses of Industry, of which the rule was *to receive all proper objects within the walls, but not to allow any thing for the relief of the out-poor, except in peculiar cases.* The directors offered to relieve the widow, by taking her seven youngest children into the house; but with great agitation of mind she refused to part with any of her children. She said she would rather die in working to maintain them, or go with all of them into the house, and work for them there. She then declared that if her landlord would continue her in the *farm*, as she called it, she would undertake to maintain and bring up all her fourteen children, without any parochial assistance.

"She was a strong woman, about forty-five years old, and of a noble undaunted spirit; happily, too, she had to do with a benevolent landlord. He told her she should continue as tenant, and hold the land the first year rent-free; and at the same time, unknown to her, he directed his receiver not to call upon her afterwards, thinking that even with that indulgence it would be a great thing if she could support so large a family.

"This further liberality, however, was not needed. By means of her two cows and of the land, she exerted herself so as to bring up all her children, twelve of whom she placed out in service; and continued to pay her rent regularly, of her own accord, every year after the first. She carried part of the milk of her cows, together with the cream and butter, to sell at Woodbridge, a market-town two miles off, and brought back bread and other necessaries ; with which, and her skim-milk and butter-milk, &c. she supported her family.

"At length, when all her children except the two younger ones were able to get their living, (and they, indeed, could almost maintain themselves), the widow gave up the land, with expressions of gratitude for the enjoyment of it, which had afforded her the means of supporting her family, under a calamity which must otherwise have driven both her and her children into a workhouse."

OBSERVATIONS BY SIR THOMAS BERNARD.

" This is an extraordinary instance of what maternal affection, assisted by a little kindness and encouragement, will do. To separate the children of the poor from their parents, is equally impolitic and unkind. It destroys the energy of the parent, and the affections and principles of the child.—Man is a creature of *wants*. From *them* are derived all our exertions, On the necessity of the infant, is founded the affection of the mother; and among the poor (I except those cases where parental affection may be chilled, and enfeebled, by extreme depression of circumstances—but, generally among the poor,) where that necessity exists in the greatest force, natural affection is the strongest. Among the rich, children are too frequently the subject either of pride or of penitence.

" The practice of supplying cottagers with cows, and with the means of feeding them, would, undoubtedly, tend to diminish the calls for parochial relief; and render unnecessary that barbarous system of removing the child from its natural, and most affectionate guardians.—The year's rent remitted, and the land confided to this poor widow, not only enabled her to support and educate her children at home, but was the means of saving the parish a very considerable expense ; as the reception and feeding and clothing of the seven youngest children, at an expense of hardly less than seventy pounds a-year, would probably have been followed by nearly an equal expense with the widow and the other children. Besides this, the encouragement of industry and good management among the poor in their cottages, and assisting them in their endeavours to thrive, would contribute to the increase of a hardy and industrious race of people ; and afford a supply to our markets of eggs, butter, poultry, pigs, garden-stuff, and almost every article of life, tending to lower the price of provisions, to prevent monopoly, and to enrich the country, both in people and produce, to a degree beyond all calculation."

EXAMPLE SECOND.—*Reports. Vol. II. p.* 290.

SIR THOS. BERNARD gives a most interesting account of an industrious cottager, whose beautiful little cottage and neat garden stand near the road-side, two miles from Tadcaster; and which have long attracted the admiration of travellers.

" His name is BRITTON ABBOT ; his age sixty-seven, and his wife's nearly the same. At nine years old, he had worked with a farmer, and being careful, and a good labourer, particularly in task work, had managed so well, that before he was twenty-two years of age, he had accumulated near 40*l*. He then married, and took a little farm at 30*l*. a-year; but before the end of the second year, he found it prudent, or rather, necessary, to quit it ; having exhausted, in his attempts to thrive upon it, almost all the little property he had heaped together.

" After this, he fixed in a cottage at Poppleton; where, with two acres of land, and his common-right, he kept two cows. He had resided here very comfortably, as a labourer, for nine years, and had six children living, and his wife preparing to lie in of a seventh, when an inclosure of Poppleton took place, and the arrangements made in consequence of it, obliged him to seek for a new habitation and other means of subsistence.

" He applied to 'Squire FAIRFAX, from whom he obtained a small slip of ground, exactly a rood, by the road-side, which he now occupies ; and with a little assistance from his neighbours, in the carriage of the materials, he built his present house, and planted the garden, inclosing it with a hedge of a single row of quick, which he cut down six times successively, when it was young, to make it grow the thicker. Mr. FAIRFAX was so much pleased with the progress of his work, and the extreme neatness of his place, that he told him he should have it *rent-free*. His answer deserves to be remembered: ' Now, Sir, you have a pleasure in seeing my cottage and garden neat: and why should not other 'Squires have the same pleasure, in seeing the cottages and gardens so nice about them? The poor would then be happy, and would love them, and the place where they lived; but now every little nook of land is to be let to the great farmers, and nothing left for the poor but to go to the parish.'

" At the age of sixty-seven, six of his children had attained to man's estate; and five of them living and thriving in the world. His eldest son has a little farm near Hemsley-Moor; one of his daughters is the wife of a joiner at York; another of them is the occupier of a little farm at Kelfield; a third is married to a labouring man, who has a little land of his own, near Dudfield; the fourth is the wife of a labourer, who has built a cottage for himself at Tadcaster, and wants nothing (as the father observed), but a bit of ground for a garden. BRITTON ABBOT says he now earns 12s. a-week, and sometimes 15s. and 18s. by hoeing turnips, setting quick, and other task-work; " But, to be sure [he added] *I have a grand character in all this country!*" He gets from his garden, annually, about 40 bushels of potatoes, besides other vegetables; and his fruit, in a good year, is worth from 3l. to 4l. His wife occasionally goes out to work; she also *spins* at home, and takes care of the garden. He says, they have lived very happy together for forty-five years. To the account that I have given, it may be needless to add, that neither he nor any part of his family, has ever had occasion to apply for parochial relief."

" On Sir THOMAS BERNARD's inquiring his *secret*, how it was he kept his cottage and garden in such neat order, he seemed pleased, and very much affected; he said ' nothing would make poor folks more happy, than to find *that great folks thought of them*; that he wished every poor man had as comfortable a home as his own; not but that he believed there might be a few *thriftless fellows*, who would not do good in it.' "

OBSERVATIONS BY SIR THOS. BERNARD.

" The history of BRITTON ABBOT appears to merit attention. At the time of the inclosure of Poppleton, when he had six young children living, and his wife preparing to lie in of a seventh, his whole little system of economy and arrangement was at once destroyed; his house, his garden, his little field, taken from him, and all his sources of wealth dried up. With less success in his application for *the rood of land*, the spot in which his industry was to be exerted, and (in justice to him it must be added,) *with less energy than he possessed, he might have gone, with his whole family into a work-house;* and from that hour have become a burden to the public, *instead of being one of its most useful members.*

" Observe, for a moment, the effects of his well-directed industry. Without any parochial aid, he has raised six of his seven children to a state of maturity, and has placed them out respectably and comfortably in the world. At the age of sixty-seven, he continued to be a good working-labourer ; happy in his own industry and good management, in the neatness and comfort of his cottage, and in the extreme fertility of his garden.

" BRITTON ABBOT possessed a degree of energy and spirit, that we must not expect to find in *every* cottager. If, however, the poor do *not* exert themselves, and have not so much forethought and management as might be wished, *the fault is less in them, than in the system of our poor-laws,* and in the *manner* in which they are executed. Were the poor properly and universally encouraged to industry and economy, we should soon find thriving and happy cottagers in every part of the kingdom. Let only a tenth part of the money now spent in workhouses, in what is called " *the relief of the poor,*" be applied in *assisting* and encouraging them to thrive and be happy in their cottages, the poor-rate would be lessened, and a national *saving* made, both in labour and food. The labourer is capable of more exertion, and is maintained for less than half the expense, in his cottage, than in a workhouse. In his cottage, he has his family around him, he has something he can call his own, he has objects to look forward to, and is the master of his own actions. *Domestic connections, property, liberty, the hope of advancement, those master-springs of human action, exist not in a workhouse.*"

As the limits of this work will not allow us to follow our excellent philanthropist through the whole of his judicious observations on this article, we shall conclude with noticing, that " the quarter of an acre which BRITTON ABBOT enclosed was not originally worth a shilling a-year; yet, by his industry, it contained, at length, a good house, and a garden abounding with fruit, vegetables, and almost every thing that constitutes the wealth of a cottager. In such inclosures, the benefit to the country, and to the individuals of the parish, would far surpass any petty sacrifice of land to be required. FIVE UNSIGHTLY, UNPROFITABLE ACRES OF WASTE GROUND WOULD AFFORD HABITATION AND COMFORT TO TWENTY SUCH FAMILIES AS BRITTON ABBOT'S ! !"

Another account of meritorious and persevering industry is given in the Reports of the "Society for bettering the Condition of the Poor;" vol. iii, p. 135, from which the following is an extract:

" JOSEPH AUSTIN, a bricklayer at Little-Shelford, near Cambridge, had often looked with a longing eye on a bit of ground by the road-side, situated on what is called the ' *Lord's Waste ;*' *and thought what a nice spot it would be for building a house on.*

And so continually was his mind occupied about it, that as soon as he fell asleep at night, he used to dream of beginning to build. At length, he applied to the Manor-Court, and got a verbal leave for that purpose. Two of his neighbours, however, moved with envy, said that if he began, they would either pull or burn it down; upon which he again applied to the Manor-Court the following year, and obtained *legal possession*, with the assent of the copyholders; paying for the entry of his name in the Court-Rolls, together with sixpence a-year, quit-rent.

"This man, when he began to build, was possessed of only *fourteen shillings* in cash! and had a wife and four children (with an increasing family) to maintain by his labour. One of his masters, however, for whom he worked, sold him an old cottage for nine guineas, the amount of which he was to work out, and which he accordingly did in about three years. With the old materials, and a quantity of *bats* composed of clay mixed with straw, and dried in the sun, like *bricks*, but not burnt, and which he had previously prepared, he laid the foundation of his intended house, in the beginning of the summer of 1791. These clay-bats make good substantial walls, provided they are secured from wet; whilst, for the foundation, and such parts of the building as would be exposed to the weather, the old bricks turned to a good account.

"After the walls were raised one story high, it was discovered that the timber of the old cottage would be too small to serve for so *large* a house as the one he had begun to build. Not overcome with this disheartening difficulty, he set about erecting a shed at the end of the building, for the reception of his wife and family, which, with great exertion, was got ready by the following autumn; and the original plan, though relinquished for the present, was afterwards proceeded in as circumstances enabled him.

"As it was necessary that this industrious man should continue to work for his masters, in order to attain the means of subsistence for his family, the time which he could devote to his favourite building was chiefly before and after the labour of the day, and by *moonlight*. He told the writer of this narrative that the clock had frequently struck 12 before he gave over his work, though he had to rise again at four, and go several miles to his daily labour, and return in the evening. Thus, by working when other men were asleep, AUSTIN had raised his walls to the second story, at the end of five years (which was in the year 1796), without any assistance excepting occasionally that of his brother. In three years after he covered in his house with pantile; but he did not consider the outside as completed until 1801, when it received the last coat of plaster: much, however, remained to be done to the inside before the building was finished.

" In this manner, with an industry and economy rarely to be met with, JOSEPH AUSTIN built himself a substantial, comfortable dwelling-house, in the space of little more than ten years, at the cost of about 50*l.* besides labour. His garden was no less the object of his attention than his house; it was neatly laid out and snugly fenced, and contained several sorts of fruit-trees, besides gooseberry and currant; it produced plenty of potatoes also, and other useful vegetables.

" But the most pleasing part of this man's history was, that he maintained a good character for honesty, sobriety, and regular attendance at church. His wife, too, though subject to ill health, was entitled to commendation for her industry, and the careful manner in which she brought up her children. Of these she had borne four during the last ten years, in addition to the first four; but had lost as many by death. As a proof of her industry, she taught her eldest son to *knit stockings;* in which he employed his time on evenings, and when not engaged in business, out of doors."

The article from which this account is drawn, was communicated by the Rev. JAMES PLUMTREE, who concludes with the following

OBSERVATIONS:

" The character of JOSEPH AUSTIN seems worthy of being held up as an example, not only to the poorer but to the richer classes of the community. It exhibits a specimen of meritorious industry and economy, shews how much a man may achieve by his own individual energy, and proves that it is not *money,* but *management,* which is the greatest requisite. For ' where there is a *will* there is always a *way;*' an honest and commendable one for the accomplishing of any good purpose.

" Without land of his own, and with only *fourteen shillings* in his pocket, JOSEPH AUSTIN began to build; and found the means not merely of building a place to shelter his family in, but of erecting an *elegant mansion,* with a garden around it, which shall continue to be his and his son's after him, and his son's son's, we hope, for many generations.

" It is true, that he possessed one advantage in his trade beyond many other men; but I see no reason why *any clever man, of any trade whatever,* may not erect a cottage upon similar principles. He might begin with small means, and get on by degrees, improving gradually in his work, until his " mansion," if not in size, at least in workmanship and appearance, might rival the one we have been describing.

" Such a house would be his *castle* while he lived, and a *monument* of his industry at his death; nay, during his life, it would display to all passers-by an instance of the extraordinary advantages of a good character for industry and ingenuity, which might vie with the sculptured marble of statesmen and warriors!!!"

6th March, 1801.

Extract from an Account of a PROVISION, ENABLING COTTAGERS TO KEEP COWS, AT HUMBERSTON, *in the County of Lincoln.*—*By* THOMAS THOMPSON, *Esq.*

" In the parish of Humberston, near Grimsby, there are **13** cottagers, all of whom are in possession respectively of the means of keeping a cow, and some of them might keep more. The whole of the parish is the property of Lord CARRINGTON. The land on which the cottages stand, with the little paddocks and gardens adjoining, contains in the whole about sixteen acres. Besides this, at the distance of a quarter of a mile from the village, there are about 60 acres of land, appropriated to the use of the cottagers. This land is divided into two plots; one of which is pasture, for the cows in summer, and the other is kept as meadow-land, to provide hay for them in winter. Each cottager knows his own piece of meadow-land, and he lays upon it all the manure which he can obtain, in order that he may have the more hay. When one of the two plots of ground has been mown for two or three years, it is then converted into the summer pasture, and the other is used as meadow-land, by which means no part of the land occupied by the cottagers is injured by constant mowing.

" The cottagers are independent of the greater farmers, holding their cottages and lands directly of Lord CARRINGTON, and not as under-tenants. This gives them a degree of respectability which they would not otherwise possess. The rent which they pay for their land is below the farmers' rent; but it is certain that, in the greatest part of this kingdom, the cottager would rejoice at being permitted to pay the utmost value given by the farmers for as much land as would keep a cow, if he could obtain it at that price.

" Lord CARRINGTON is the patron of the living of Humberston; and, upon the last vacancy, he gave it to a respectable and conscientious clergyman, who has exerted himself very strenuously in the religious and moral improvement of his parishioners. He has laboured with great and good effect. The cottagers are sober and industrious, and it is not known that any man in the parish lives in a course of habitual immorality. The Clergyman, with Lord CARRINGTON's assistance, has also succeeded in establishing, for the benefit of the youth at Humberston, a *parish school*, which has been of very essential service to the parish.

" There is no public-house at Humberston, nor do the parishioners desire one; and, on this account, there are no cock-fightings or gamings within the parish, nor any drunken-meetings for the purpose of settling the parish rates. The poor-rates in the parish of Humberston, which include the charges for the families of the men serving in the militia, never amount to more than ninepence or ten-pence in the pound on the rental, and are, generally, under sixpence."

OBSERVATIONS.

" The reduction of the poor-rates, the increase of the comforts, and the improvement of the religious and moral habits of the poor, in the parish of Humberston, may be fairly ascribed to the circumstances above stated. The publication of the letter of the Earl of Winchelsea, on the expediency and benefit of letting small quantities of land to cottagers, to enable them to keep cows, will, I trust, be of the greatest use to the country. Exclusive of the benevolence and charity of thus adding to the comforts of the poor, advantages of the utmost importance must be derived from such a system by the *land-owners* and *farmers* themselves. It is essential to every farmer, that there should be a sufficient number of labourers in his neighbourhood to enable him to occupy his land to the greatest advantage, otherwise he cannot afford to pay a fair and full rent for his land, and manage his farm in a manner beneficial to himself and to his landlord. Those labourers who have no local advantage of situation, no tie of property, nor any appropriate benefit to attach them to a particular spot, are inclined to wander up and down a country, without any connexion, and are always ready to change their employer for a trifling advance in their wages; whereas those cottagers who have the advantage of property, who possess a cow, and rent a little ground, are the persons on whose assistance the farmer may depend in the time of necessity, and on whose honesty and ability he may implicitly rely."*

On Cottagers' keeping Cows.
By the Bishop of Durham.

" Among the cottagers on Lord WINCHELSEA's estate, in the county of Rutland, which I have lately visited, I have selected for the Society three examples of the benefit of cottagers' renting land. They are as follows:

---

* " Reports" of the " Society for bettering the Condition of the Poor;" vol. ii. page 231.

"A day-labourer, his wife, and eight small children.—An old man of fourscore, and his wife of nearly the same age.—And an old single woman.

"The first and second of these families have each two cows, and the old single woman has one cow, with land to keep them on. They have each of them gardens. With this benefit, and that of his labour, the day-labourer has bred up ten children, two of whom are put out to service, and he is now maintaining himself, his wife, and his other eight children, *without any call for parochial relief.* The two old people cannot make any thing of their labour; but yet, with the benefit of their cow and garden, and the exertions which these call forth, and with a little occasional assistance that the old man and his wife receive from their son, and that which the other old woman has from her younger neighbours, they all appear to enjoy much more comfort than old-age in general possesses. They satisfied me that, but for the cow and the garden, they could not have subsisted without parochial relief."

OBSERVATIONS.

"I have selected these three examples from many similar ones on the same estate, in proof of the utility of the measures which Lord WINCHELSEA has adopted for the benefit of his cottagers. There are two circumstances which I learnt upon inquiry, and which I think will shew that the benefit I have stated was not local or partial, but diffused over his estate: one is, that the rate collected for the relief of the poor, in his three parishes, is not so much, on an average, as *an annual sixpence in the pound;* the other, that his cottagers' rents (for their cottages and little closes of ground) are, of all his rents, the *earliest* and *best paid,* and that there has been no arrear of them for several years.

"There was an air of content and gratitude marked in the countenances, and expressed in the language of all the cottagers, which convinced me that what had been done for them by their landlord had not only made them more happy, and improved their means of subsistence, but that it had produced very beneficial effects on the *heart* and *morals.* The advantages, however, are not confined to the *poor man and his family: they extend to the parish,* and prevent its being burthened with a heavy poor's rate; and to the *community at large,* on account of the children of the lower classes of the people being educated in habits of industry and good order, and having, at an early age, a spirit and energy infused into them by the examples of their parents, which teach them that their best and surest dependence in future life will be *on their own exertions and good conduct,* for the maintenance and welfare of themselves and their families."*

---

* "Reports" of the Society for the Poor; vol. i. p. 98.

Extract from a further Account of the ADVANTAGES *of* COTTAGERS' KEEPING COWS.—*By* SIR THOS. BERNARD, *Bart.*

" A late visit into Rutlandshire has given me an opportunity of acquiring more minute and correct information, respecting the circumstances and situation of the cottagers keeping cows, in the four parishes of Hambledon, Egleton, Greetham, and Burley-on-the-Hill. I give the result of my enquiries; and I give it with more precision and detail than I otherwise should, as I am very desirous of enabling land-owners to ascertain whether, in their own peculiar instances, it will not answer for them to follow the example of what has been done in that neighbourhood. At the same time I beg leave to anticipate the observation, that in arable countries, where there is a scarcity of grass land, and in those districts where, from vicinage to a town or a market, grass land bears a rent above its intrinsic value, it may not be practicable to supply cottagers with pasture for a cow, without some sacrifice on the part of the landlord.

" Among the tenants of this part of the estate, there are 80 cottagers who keep cows. Of those who possess cows, there are 22, each of whom has only one cow; 35 who have each 2 cows, 13 who have 3, 7 who have 4, and 3 who have 5 cows each; making in all 174 cows. Of these cottagers, about a third part have all their land in severalty; the rest of them have the use of a cow-pasture, in common with others; most of them possessing a small homestead, adjoining to their cottage; every one of them having a good garden, and keeping one pig at least, if not more. Without any exception, they pay for their land the same rent* as a farmer would, and not more.

" The estate is tithe-free. In Hambledon there is a close of 114 acres, which is let in 108 cowgates, at one guinea each; of these 74 are let to cottagers, and the remaining 34 (not having been as yet applied for by cottagers) are for the present let to farmers. The tenants have the right of feeding each four sheep, instead of a cow, for each cowgate; and the farmers generally so use their holdings, which is more for their own convenience, as well as for the general

---

* " I add a note, on the suggestion of Mr. KENT, of Fulham, who had the merit of laying the cases of the English cottager before the public, several years ago, in a very useful publication, entitled ' Hints to Gentlemen of Landed Property.' The obvious reason [Mr. KENT observes] why the cottager succeeds better with his cow upon Lord WINCHELSEA's estate is, that he is not charged a higher rent for his land than a farmer would be : but that this is far from being the case in general; so far, indeed, that there is not one instance in ten, of those in which a cottager possesses the means of keeping a cow, that he does not obtain the land from the farmer at second-hand, and at a rent at least double of what he ought to pay." *2d Nov.* 1799.

benefit of the pasture. Each of the cottagers has also an acre or more of homestead near his cottage, for which he pays a farmers' rent.

" At Egleton there is a cow pasture of only 30 acres, which is let in 26 cowgates, each at 30s. These are all occupied by cottagers, who have also small homesteads near their houses, to supply them with hay.—In the parish of Burley, the mode of providing for some of the cottagers' cows is different : a close of 11½ acres is divided into two equal parts, and the whole jointly occupied by four cottagers. One half is, every alternate year, held in four several parts by a marked boundary, each mowing his own part for hay; the other half is a cow pasture for the four cottagers. They have each a right of putting in a cow and two sheep in the pasture part during the summer, and of feeding a cow and four sheep upon the whole in the winter. The benefit of the sheep-feeding they can let to a farmer at a guinea and a half a year. Besides this, they have grass and hay for one cow; for rent, they pay 4l. 10s. a-year each, and in poor's rates and other levies, 5s. a-year, making in the whole 4l. 15s.; from which, after deducting 1l. 11s. 6d. (which their sheep-feeding is worth), there remains 3l. 3s. 6d. rent and taxes, for the support of their cow.

" The accommodation that the cottager has for his cow in Greetham is not so beneficial to him. A pasture field of 35 acres of indifferent land, worth about 10s. an acre, is held as a joint pasture by 14 cottagers, each of whom has a right to pasture a cow in it. For their winter provision they have each of them an arable field of six acres, in which they grow some clover and sainfoin. This is by no means so advantageous to them as grass land : under these circumstances, however, they are very glad to have the land, and always pay their rent with great regularity.

" I said that the cottagers paid a farmers' rent for their land, and not more; but I ought to add, that the whole of the estate is let at moderate rents. The reader may find, by calculation, that in Hambledon the land produces per acre nearly 20s.; in Egleton, about 23s.; and in Burley, 31s. per acre ; the difference being occasioned partly by the difference of time when the closes were respectively let at their present rents, and partly by some difference in the quality of the land.

" The cottagers who keep cows are almost all of them labourers in husbandry: there are, however, among them, some widows and daughters of deceased labourers, and some men who work as country carpenters, or at similar trades. I can add, that of all the rents of the estate, none are *more punctually paid than those for the cottagers' land.* The steward informs me that there has never been an instance of an arrear, or of a delay in payment, even for a few days!!

"When I state that the land is let at, and not under, a fair, moderate rent, I do not mean to be understood to say exactly the same of the cottages;* which are comfortable and habitable buildings, in good repair, neatly kept, and regularly white-washed, and yet pay no more rent than the ruinous and miserable hovels in England usually do.

"The reader may perhaps wish to know how the cottager is at first set up with a cow. As an example, I will give the history of one man who had a wife and several children, and was last year likely to be burthensome to the parish. It was agreed that the one remedy that promised relief to the parish in this case was the cottager's cow. His landlord supplied him with land at a fair rent, and made his cottage and out-buildings comfortable. He asked assistance of his neighbours: in the mansion-house he collected about two or three guineas; among the farmers, by gift or loan, he obtained some handsome additions: he purchased his cow, took possession of his land, and is now doing very well.—About eight years ago, another labourer, with a large family, was supplied with a cow and land in the same manner. He has since bred up his large family without any parochial assistance, and is now possessed of two cows, the second purchased wholly from his savings. Two others were provided with cows and land, in the like manner, about four years ago, and have gone on very well.

"The cottagers have, very generally, more than one cow each. The fact is, that in every instance, as soon as the cottager has got a cow, all the efforts of the family are directed to the attainment of the means to purchase another, and another; so that some of them who began very lately with only one, have now five cows. The chief inconvenience to be apprehended from such an increase in their property is, that they may be induced to look to the produce of their cows and gardens, for the sole support of themselves and

---

* "The increase of price in the materials for building, particularly in that country, makes it impracticable to supply the cottager with a proper and habitable dwelling, at a rent adapted to his circumstances, without some sacrifice on the part of the landlord. What remedy can be proposed for the evil, I am not aware; unless I may hope that the land-owner will some day sit down, and precisely calculate in how many ways the extra expense would be made up to him—in the general benefit and credit of his estate; in the health and well-being of the poor, and the consequent reduction of the poor-rates; in the beauty and pleasure of the country so adorned; and in self-satisfaction and real gratification. If he would enter dispassionately, and without prejudice, into this investigation, I trust he would soon discover *his true interest*; and be induced to send a few of the materials intended for his *grottos, castles,* and *temples,* to be applied to the repair of his cottages, for the credit and advantage of himself and his estates, and for the welfare and comfort of the poor connected with, and dependent on him."

their families, and cease to depend on their daily labour for their support; being thus transformed from opulent thriving labourers into little starving farmers. But the fact is directly the reverse. Such are the beneficial effects of early and steady habits of industry, that these proprietors of cows are the most steady and trusty labourers. As a proof of the effects of this system in promoting industry and frugality, I give the history of one of them, CHRISTOPHER LOVE,* of Hambledon: who is now 75 years of age, and has for 53 years past kept three cows: he has, nevertheless, gone regularly every summer, for these 50 years, to harvest-work in Cambridgeshire, because he is more in request there, and receives better wages, than he would at home. He has bred up a family of nine children in great comfort, is now in good health himself, and has been in Cambridgeshire this preceding harvest; but thinks he shall go no more, as the family for whom he used to work are all dead or removed.

"I saw one instance among them of a man who was bringing up and supporting nine children, all healthy, well-fed, clean, and neatly dressed. A little child, under four years of age, was asked if she could spin? 'No, she was too little; but she could knit.' 'Her sister [said the mother, pointing to another girl, between five and six years years of age] spins very well; she got a prize for spinning this year, and brought home a premium of the value of six shillings in clothing.'

"The training of their children to husbandry, to the management of cattle and of a dairy, and to every occupation that can fit them for the service of a farmer, is a very important advantage in this system: and if there were no other benefit to be derived from it, but that of adapting, and habitually preparing, the rising generation for the most useful and necessary employment in the island, this alone would produce an abundant compensation for any effort or attention that has been or may be directed to the subject. They are not only stout, healthy, clean, well clothed, and brought up in regular and principled habits of living, but they are used to almost every part of their business from the earliest period of their existence; every inhabitant of the cottage being, from infancy, so in-

* "Since I was at Burley, one of these owners of cows, a shepherd, of the name of Watkin, who lives within two or three doors of Christopher Love's cottage, had the misfortune to dislocate his hip. Upon his being visited, he expressed regret at the expense of his surgeon's attendance, for which he is paying half-a-guinea a visit. 'However [he added], if it pleases GOD I recover my health and strength, I shall not grudge any expense attending my cure.' In a common parish, such a circumstance would have entailed a great and continuing charge on the parish. In this instance, the sufferer never thought of applying to the parish for any assistance; and in all probability (whether a perfect cure be effected or not, which is very doubtful) he will never have any occasion for it.—10th Dec. 1799."

terested in the care of the cow, the pig, the sheep, and the garden, as to acquire at a very early age all the requisite information and practice on those subjects.

"The cottagers in this country eat barley or mixed bread; and they prefer it, for a reason which one of them gave me—that not only they can afford to have more of it, but can also add a little bit of meat to dress with the vegetables from the garden. This makes, in the aggregate, a very important amelioration in the condition of the cottager: bread, butter, cheese, plenty of milk and vegetables, and some meat to mix with their other food, compose, altogether, a table of diet unknown to many English cottagers, and extremely conducive to health, strength, and rational habits of living. It is no inconsiderable convenience to the inhabitants of this neighbourhood, that the cottagers are enabled to supply them, at a very moderate price, with milk, cream, butter, poultry, pig-meat, and veal; articles which, in general, are not worth the farmer's attention, and which therefore are supplied by speculators, who greatly enhance their price to the public.

OBSERVATIONS.

"In preparing this detail, I have endeavoured to give every circumstance as coolly and correctly as I could; being aware that, in practical information, precision is of the utmost importance. I will not, however, presume to say, that in what I have written I have been entirely uninfluenced by the desire of seeing the English cottager, what, in a free, a prosperous, and an enlightened country, he ought to be,—*thriving, industrious, and happy.*

"What has been stated will probably suggest to the reader, that the welfare of the cottager depends more on his improved resources and habits of life, than on any increase or superabundance of wages. In countries where wages are at the highest rate, without any improved system of management and economy among the poor, the condition of the cottager is very inferior to that in many places, where the wages of labour are lower, but the means and habits of life superior. Mechanics, who earn from a guinea to two guineas a-week, in London, Manchester, and other places, and who depend upon the neighbouring shop for the necessaries of life, and (to use a common expression) *live from hand to mouth,* do in general possess a less degree of domestic comfort, and enjoy a less proportion of the advantages of civilized life, than many cottagers. The explication is obvious. The mechanic, who with his family exists in a lodging, without any advantage or impulse tending to domestic economy, and who earns, by a species of *sleight of hand* in his trade, very high wages, applies what is barely necessary, by weekly payments, to the baker, and some other tradesmen, for the support of the family;

the rest goes to the club or the alehouse, or is lost in the intervals of labour: while the rural labourer and his family, who have the power and inducement to thrift and management, direct every effort to the improvement of their circumstances and the increase of their comforts.

" It will, to the latest period of my life, be a source of enviable satisfaction to me, if what is said in this and the other Reports of the Society shall have the effect of awakening the attention of the land-owner to an object so interesting and essential to him, as the situation of his industrious labourers, whose comforts and means of life he may greatly increase, not only without any immediate loss, but with a real and accumulating benefit to himself and his property: he would soon find, that, by improving the condition of his dependents, and by exciting industry among them, he must proportionally increase the value of his estate. It would, indeed, be an act not only of benevolence and justice, but of wisdom and prudence, whether he directed his views to his own insulated property or to the general welfare of the community.—Viewed in a political light, the labourer who has property, however small,— a cow, a pig, or even the crop of his garden,—has an interest in the welfare and tranquillity of his country, and in the good order of society. He who has no property, is always ready for novelty and experiment; and though gibbets and halters may for a time deter him from criminal and atrocious acts, yet no motive exists to fix him in virtuous habits, or to attach him to that national prosperity in which he has no part, and to that constituted order of property which excludes him from all possession.

" There is another consideration of advantage, suggested by the present high price of wheat corn. Those measures for the relief and subsistence of the poor, which are now essential to their existence in many other parts of the kingdom, are unnecessary in the neighbourhood of Burley. The cottager who is in the habit of using barley in bread, who keeps a pig, perhaps two, and has plenty of milk and vegetables, has within his power almost all the means of life; and feels very little inconvenience from that which, in the present season, without the charitable aid and attention of the opulent, would oppress and overwhelm the labourer whose existence depends on a mere pecuniary stipend. With such means of life, he is less affected by the present high price of bread than almost any other individual: the dearness of provisions produces not much variation in his circumstances, except by delaying, for a very short time, the desired period of his purchasing another cow, and by retarding his progressive thrift, and the improvement of his little property, for the benefit and *hereditary succession* of his wife and children.

"In the facility of execution, and the permanence of effect, a very material difference exists between measures taken for the improvement of the cottager's means of life *in his own cottage,* and

the increase of his resources and incitements to thrift and industry, and those for the support and conduct of all *public charities
and establishments* for the relief of the poor. The latter require
an unceasing continuance of exertion, and an unfailing perseverance
in disinterested care and attention; the former executes itself. The
latter measures provide for the maintenance and relief of helpless and
hopeless dependents; the former produce the *restoration* of health
and strength. When the cottager has acquired, and feels the benefit
of his new resources and habits of life, his own exertions, his own
attentions, will provide for the continuance of the blessings of his
family, as long as his landlord will protect him in the enjoyment
of his cottage and ground. He requires, in this instance, no subsequent care or attention, on the part of his benefactor, to prevent the
return of indigence and misery; whereas it demands the continuance of unwearied exertion in all public establishments, to conduct
them properly, for the solace and relief of existing wretchedness.

"In all that has been done by the Earl of WINCHELSEA for his
cottagers, though there has been much attention paid, and much
disposition on his part to make a very considerable sacrifice, if
requisite, for their benefit, yet, in fact, and with the single exception
which I have stated as to his cottages, so far from any loss or expense
being incurred by him, a considerable and permanent improvement
has been made upon his estate, without any reduction in the immediate profit. While the land let to the cottager is set at the same
rent as that which the farmers occupy, the country is enriched and
improved by an industrious and thriving tenantry, and the poor-
rates reduced to almost nothing.* The labourer's children are at
the same time so bred up, and so accustomed to regular habits
of employment, as to be very little burthensome to their parents, and
a great and improving benefit to the estate. The land-owner
should keep in mind, that if the labourer be reduced to indigence,
his support, which had been derived from his own exertions, must,
in future, be drawn from the land. The farmer, indeed, *nominally*
pays the poor-rate; but it is *really and ultimately defrayed by the
landlord;* whose estate, by the increase and accumulation of poor-
rate, is deteriorated in value, and diminished in rental: while, on
the contrary, by a different system,—by promoting the welfare, and
encouraging the energy of the cottager,—the land-owner might have

---

* In confirmation of what is here stated, I have much pleasure in adding
an extract from a letter of Mr. Bassett, of Glentworth, in Lincolnshire, to
Mr. Arthur Young, dated 6th Aug. 1799:—" On this and on other estates
belonging to Lord Scarborough, his Lordship has invariably directed me to
accommodate the cottagers with a sufficient quantity of land to keep from one
to two cows, and no more; allotting as much meadow to each of such cottagers
as will keep their cattle with hay in the winter season; and I am convinced,

lessened the poor-rate, and augmented the value and rental of his land.

"I do not mean to assert, that the English cottager, narrowed as he now is in his means and habits of living, may be immediately capable of taking that active and useful station in society which is filled by those who are the subject of this paper. To produce so great an improvement in his character and circumstances, would require time and attention. The cottager, however, in this part of the county of Rutland, is *not of a different species from other English cottagers;* and if he had not been protected and encouraged by his landlord, he would have been the same helpless and comfortless creature that we see in some other parts of England. The farmer (with the assistance of the steward) would have taken his land; the creditor, his cow and pig; and the workhouse, his family.

"As I am disposed to flatter myself that some of my readers, who have landed property adapted to the experiment, *may* be induced to try this mode of *improving their estates,* I shall suggest what occurs to me as the proper method of proceeding: premising that, in this and in every thing else which the landlord may think fit to do for the benefit of his cottagers, he should be extremely careful not to make them the subjects of jealousy or dislike, to either the farmer or shopkeeper; on whose good-will to them, in spite of every attention of the landlord, much of their comfort and well-being will depend, particularly in winter, when the presence of a friend and protector is most wanted. I should therefore advise him, at first, to follow the example of Mr. BURDON, and to begin with a close or two of the ground in his own occupation. Let him then select two or three of his most thriving and industrious labourers, and inform each of them that he is disposed to accommodate him with a little ground, at a moderate rent, if he can contrive to get a cow, and his wife can manage her; adding the offer of a small loan or donation towards it. The introduction of so novel a system may possibly require some aid and attention at first; and it may be proper that the poor-rate on their ground should be kept down as low as it may fairly be: but as soon as two or three cottagers have succeeded, and it is known that upon land becoming vacant in future the cottager will be con-

---

from the experience of 30 years, during which time I have been agent to the Scarborough family, that the result has been highly conducive to the happiness of my poor neighbours, and advantageous to the occupiers of farms, who have always a set of *industrious labourers* within their respective parishes, *who do not become chargeable in the time of sickness,* or when, from age, manual labour cannot be any longer performed by them: at such periods the produce of their cows and gardens afford them the means of a decent maintenance, and the regular discharge of their rents. I make out, yearly, the accounts of this parish; and the rates and assessments on the occupiers of land do not on the average amount to more than *eightpence in the pound,* for the poor, church, constable, and highways."

sidered as well as the farmer, though not to the injury or inconvenience of the latter ; and that, upon the occupier of any little farm of
20 or 30 acres being obliged, as it frequently happens, to abandon a
losing concern, the landlord would, in some instances, be disposed
to divide the ground for the accommodation of five or six of his most
deserving and thriving labourers ; the farmer would soon be reconciled to a system which must in its nature operate to lower the poor-
rate, and diminish the burthen of the poor : the character of the
cottager would be invigorated ; his spirit, his industry, his economy
would be all put in action ; and a very essential improvement would
take place in the estate and neighbourhood.

"22d Oct. 1799."   *Reports;* vol. ii. p. 169.

Cottagers' Gardens.

The accommodating of industrious and deserving day-labourers
with plots of ground for the purpose of raising potatoes and other
vegetables, has proved (in places where it has been tried) highly
beneficial to the community. It has encouraged a spirit of industry
and self-support among the labouring classes, whose morals have
thereby been improved, and their comforts increased. Besides
which, the advantages of such a practice to landholders are so evident, that one might suppose they would see it their interest to promote it in every parish, as a means of reducing the poor-rates.

These gardens should be large enough to produce plenty of
roots for the cottager's family, but not so extensive as to tempt him
to withdraw his attention from his daily labour for his master, nor
to make his produce much of an article of sale. In the spring,
when the potatoes are to be planted, not only does the father of the
family give all his spare time to his garden, if he have one, mornings
and evenings, in the dusk or by moon-light, but his wife, and such of
their children as are capable of labour, are employed in digging the
ground and putting in the potatoes. It is an interesting season to
the whole family, whose hopes and future comfort depend much
upon the degree of industry and good management which is exerted
at this time ; and though further exertion is necessary until the
planting and hoeing are over, an hour or two in a day is sufficient
for the general purposes afterwards.

Although the principal part of a cottager's garden should necessarily be appropriated to the culture of *potatoes,* on which the chief
support of his family, and of his *pig* too (if he keep one), is to
depend ; yet vegetables and other useful roots ought not to be
overlooked, such as carrots, parsnips, turnips, leeks, onions, beans,
&c. (peas, however, if sticks are to be provided, are a less profitable
crop to a poor man.)

We are supposing the average size of a labourer's garden to be about half an acre; but in situations where more land than this can be obtained, and where a man and his family may be able properly to manage more, grain and other things should be cultivated. In the vicinity of London, and in various parts of the country, a man may advantageously cultivate one, two, or three acres of land, chiefly by spade-husbandry: by judiciously changing his crops, from corn to clover, lucerne, or other artificial grasses, and afterwards to potatoes, turnips, carrots, or similar roots, the ground produces more, by this means, without being exhausted, than if such changes were not adopted.

The following account is given by Sir HENRY VAVASOUR, in in the 3d vol. of the Reports for the Poor, p. 329, of a man's cultivating three acres of arable land in Yorkshire, by this species of *field-gardening*, at an annual profit of 10*l*. per acre:

Produce.	Value.			Land.		
	£.	s.	d.	A.	R.	P.
240 bushels of potatoes	24	0	0	0	2	0
60 ditto of carrots	6	0	0	0	1	0
5 quarters of oats, at 44s. per. qr.	11	0	0	0	3	20
4 loads of clover, part hay, part cut green .... }	12	0	0	1	0	10
Turnips	1	0	0	0	0	20
In garden-stuff for the family, viz. beans, peas, cabbages, leeks, &c. }	0	0	0	0	0	30
	£54	0	0	Acres 3	0	3

	£.	s.	d.	Produce before stated. £.	s.	d.
Deduct rent, including the house, seeds, &c. ...... }	9	0	0	54	0	0
Value of labour	10	10	0	Expenses 23	2	0
	£23	2	0	Profit £30	18	0

if sold at market, exclusive of butter, the sale of which was equal to the rent, besides a little being retained for the use of the family.

"His stock was two* cows and two pigs. The land was partly ploughed, and partly dug with a spade; the digging was performed by the man, his wife, and a girl about 12 years of age, at *spare* hours from their daily *hired* work, the profits of which nearly supported them; nor did they often quit their employers' work for a whole day together, excepting in harvest.

---

* The man's cows were kept, generally, during the year, on the produce of the land, except that one of them had a summer's *gait* for twenty weeks with his landlord.

"A profit of 30*l*. per annum upon three acres of land was certainly more than could have been made by a farmer on a large scale. But this was a case of extraordinary industry.

"It is stated that the family lived well; that the man, by his economy, had been enabled to place out two sons in good situations, and to lay by something handsome every year besides."

Dated May, 1801.

The benefit to individuals, and to the community, derived from accommodating industrious cottagers with small portions of land for gardens, at a moderate rent, is so happily described in the 15th vol. of the *Quarterly Review*, p. 207, that we shall present our readers with the following extract:

"The experiment was tried also in Wiltshire, in a parish containing 140 poor persons, divided into 32 families, chiefly employed as labourers in husbandry. Having suffered greatly during the high price of provisions in 1801, it was proposed to them that they should make an effort to better their circumstances, and occupy, at a fair rent, such a quantity of land as each family could cultivate without improperly interfering with their usual labour, and keep it well manured. The land was to be forfeited if they received any relief from the parish, except medical assistance, or under the militia laws. The proposal was gladly accepted by all who could possibly accept it; and the consequence was, that the poor-rates, which, in the last six months before the experiment was made, had amounted to 212*l*. 16*s*., amounted, three years afterwards, in the six corresponding months of winter, only to 12*l*. 6*s*.! Some part of this great difference is, of course, attributable to the scarcity in the first year; but the fact, that *all* the sefamilies had been chargeable to the parish, and that *none of them were chargeable after they had been thus enabled to assist themselves,* proves incontestably that no better means can be devised for improving the condition of the agricultural poor. The utmost quantity of land thus leased was an acre and a half to each, of which a fourth part was planted with *potatoes;* the rest was in corn, or in garden cultivation: and this experiment shews that even arable land is not always hurtful to the cottager.

"Of all means of improving the husbandman's condition, this has been found the most beneficial. The children are thus educated to husbandry, to gardening, or to the care of catttle. While they are thus healthfully and usefully brought up, they are better fed; the father employs those hours in hopeful, and therefore willing occupation, which would otherwise be idly or injuriously spent, and finds such solid satisfaction at the close of the day by his own fireside, that the alehouse holds out no temptation to him; and the mother has that enjoyment in her offspring which, in the right order of things, has been appointed by a benevolent Creator, instead of feeling, as is too often the unnatural state of the miserably poor, that their existence is burthensome to their parents, and calamitous to themselves.

"The individual *Christian*, if he truly deserve that name, will ever bear in mind an humiliating sense of the evil propensities of fallen humanity, as a motive for vigilance over his own heart, and for charity towards the offences of others. But it is the business of *Governments* to regard the bright side of human nature: the better they think of mankind, the better will they find them, and the better they will make them. It is well known that in the middle and higher walks of life, men in general bear adverse fortune more wisely than they bear prosperity. One reason for this is, that these opposite states call into action the same principle; and pride, which makes man insolent or arrogant in one situation, is in the other chastened and refined till it becomes a virtue. The wisest and the best minds have received their painful education in the school of adversity: but if adversity be favourable to the development of our virtues (and indeed many of our noblest qualities would never be developed under any other discipline), *there is a degree of misery which is fatal to them, and which hardens the heart as much as coarse manual labour indurates the skin, and destroys all finer sense of touch.* Among savages, those tribes have ever been found the most unfeeling, who possess the fewest comforts, and have the most difficulty in obtaining food; for when self-preservation becomes the prime concern, the natural charities are starved; a brutish selfishness occupies the whole heart, and man, having no instinct to supply the absence of human affections, becomes worse than the beasts. Mournful as this is, it is far more mournful to contemplate the effects of *extreme poverty in the midst of a civilized and flourishing society.* The wretched native of Terra-del-Fuego, or of the northern extremity of America, sees nothing around him which aggravates his own wretchedness *by comparison:* the chief fares no better than the rest of the horde, and the slave no worse than the master; the privations which they endure are common to all, they know of no state happier than their own, and submit to their miserable circumstances as to the law of nature. But in a country like ours, there exists a contrast which continually forces itself upon the eye and upon the reflective faculty."

In page 209 the subject is thus continued:

"From the moment when the man begins to think that 'The world is not his friend, nor the world's law,' the world and the world's law are likely to have that man for their enemy; and if he does not commence direct hostilities against them, he abandons himself to despair, and becomes a useless if not a hurtful member of the community. Attempts to reclaim him by penal statutes are worse than unavailing. They provoke that spirit of stubbornness which, oftentimes, is only the disease that ill treatment and untoward circumstances produce in a noble disposition. You might as well attempt to stop the progress of contagion by punishing all who are affected by the baneful principles in the air, as to remedy poverty by penal laws against the poor."

"Laws," says Sir Thomas Bernard, "have been made to *compel* men to industry and economy, and workhouses have been erected and *farmed* to the best bidder, in order to *deter* the poor from *wanting relief;* but parishes and parish officers have not as yet been aware, that in every instance in which a poor family is driven by distress to take refuge in a workhouse, *an incumbrance has been entailed on the funds of the parish, never to be redeemed even in part, except by a change of system; namely, by* Encouraging *that industry and prudence which no* act of parliament *can* compel; and by assisting them with increased means and advantages of life, calculated to enable them to support themselves and their families in their own cottages, without parochial relief."

It is gratifying to learn that, in different parts of the country, parish officers, and others concerned in the relief of the Poor, appear to be fully convinced of the expediency and sound policy of supplying industrious labourers with *garden plots*, as a means of reducing the poor-rates; and that they have, in some instances, proceeded to rent land, and parcel it out in potatoe-gardens among the labourers in their respective parishes.

On the Advantage of Cottagers' keeping a Pig.

The benefits derived by individuals, as well as the community at large, by accommodating industrious labourers with the means of keeping a *cow*, have been clearly demonstrated in the foregoing chapters. There is, however, another source of profit which remains to be noticed, that of keeping a *pig*, or a few geese, if these labourers happen to be situated near a common.

Although it may be found impracticable in some parts of the kingdom to furnish the means of keeping a cow, the same objections will not apply to keeping a pig; provided a plot of garden-ground, for raising potatoes, &c. be attainable.

To a labourer who is possessed of a tolerably large garden and a pig, and still more if a cow be added to his stock, a cheering prospect arises of improved means of subsistence, and of increased comforts. The advantage is not to be estimated merely by the pecuniary profit which he derives, but by the superior tone of industry and saving which cannot fail to be produced in the man's general conduct; for when habits of application and economy have been once acquired, and their fruits enjoyed, they generally continue to be a blessing to the possessor through life, and his own good example is handed down to his children after him. Such a man possesses an object to which all his hopes and wishes are directed; his energies are thus excited, he becomes attached to his condition, and is reconciled to a life of labour and hardship.

The means of keeping a pig are not confined to the cottager's *garden;* if he lives near a town, he may get malt-grains, and the refuse of kitchens, " pigs' wash;" and in harvest time his pig may pick up a great deal of waste corn in the highways: besides which, the barley, oats, peas, &c. that a woman and her children may glean in the fields, would keep a pig in good condition. In addition to these means, industrious hands may collect in the woods, in the fall of the year, abundance of acorns, beech masts, &c. which afford excellent food for pigs.

A considerable advantage to be derived from a pig is the manure which it affords: this, when mixed with scrapings of the highways, or other soil which might be collected from the habitations of even the poorest people, will tend much to fertilize the garden.

Near some towns where horses employed in stagecoaches are kept and fed highly, and a good deal of travelling takes place, it is pleasing to observe numbers of industrious children engaged in collecting the horse-dung which falls, and affords sufficient manure for the garden of many a poor family.

" JAMES BRAMSGROVE, a farmer's labourer, having saved by his industry the sum of four guineas, purchased a hog, and put it up to fatten in April. In the course of fattening, three quarters and a half of beans, and seven bushels of peas, were used; which were obtained chiefly on credit, from his master and others. He had a wife and five children; the two eldest, girls, not exceeding twelve years old. He and his wife and two girls earned, during the harvest, 2l. 2s. per week; and in one week the industrious family earned 2l. 11s.; which enabled them not only to maintain themselves decently, but to pay for the fattening of the pig. The hog was killed at Michaelmas, and weighed 64st. 3lb.; part of it sold at 7½d. per lb. and the rest was reserved for the use of the family. Estimating the whole at 7½d. per lb. the value of the hog would have been above 16l.; but as what was sold consisted of the prime pieces, some deduction ought to be made on that account."*

---

* " Reports" of the " Society for bettering the Condition of the Poor;" vol. i. page 158.

On the Keeping of Bees.

THE pleasing descriptions given by Eastern writers, sacred and profane, of countries abounding with "milk and honey," naturally convey to our minds the agreeable ideas of *plenty* and *comfort*. When we read of "a land flowing with milk and honey," our imagination represents to us a country of extraordinary fertility, affording all things necessary for the comfort and support of life.

In several of the foregoing chapters, we have endeavoured to encourage a renewed attempt to furnish our peasants with the means of keeping a cow wherever it can be done; and now we earnestly recommend to the friends of industrious cottagers, to promote, as much as possible, the keeping of Bees.

This branch of rural economy requires but little attention or capital. A few shillings are sufficient to *purchase* hives, even though labourers should not possess ingenuity enough to construct them at home, at leisure hours, in wet weather, or on winter evenings.

The bountiful hand of Nature furnishes all the ingredients for the rich store with which these diligent insects supply us. It is not necessary that the owner of bees should possess either land or meadows, or even a flower-garden; neither sowing nor reaping, nor any toil of man, is required.

The sagacious bee, guided by unerring instinct, needs no human agency to direct her course, but explores the flowery meadows, fields, and commons, at great distances from her hive, in search of Nature's sweets; and, after collecting as much honey or wax as she is able to carry, returns home loaded, by the same wonderful direction!

The poorest cottager, therefore, may keep bees, provided he possess a commodious station for depositing the hives, where they will be secure from high winds, rain, and other annoyances. No sort of filth should be allowed to collect near the dwellings of these delicate insects, whose sense of smelling is so exquisisely fine as not to endure fœtid smells. Nor should weeds or grass be permitted to grow near the hives, so as to harbour snails, slugs, or insects; but they should be occasionally inspected, in order to detect the inroads of spiders, mice, or vermin of any kind.

A good stock, or hive of bees, well filled with honey and wax, would be worth from 25s. to 30s. The writer of this has counted twenty hives in a peasant's garden: but though the whole number of these could not be expected to be equally filled with treasure, he thinks that one good stock out of four (if the summer has been favourable) might fairly be reckoned on to be taken at Michaelmas.

Means have been suggested by the curious for taking the honey and wax without destroying the bees; but we fear the process which they recommend would not come within the capacity of poor cottagers. Besides, it may happen that, after taking away a part of the honey in summer, the bees would starve in winter, except they were fed.

We do not pretend, in this summary way, to give the natural history of bees, or practical directions for their management. For such information we respectfully refer the ingenious reader to WILDMAN or HUISH, who have both written on the subject. The cottager, whose interest we have in view, will be at little loss in gaining information on all necessary points in almost every country village. Our object is merely to suggest additional resources, and to excite the higher classes of society to promote, by all possible means, the improvement of the condition of industrious persons in the lower ranks of life, in order that they may once more be brought nearer to the level of comparative comfort to which by nature they are entitled, as well as the rich.

Employment in the Fisheries, as affected by the Salt Duties.

THERE remains to be noticed one more source of employment for the POOR; perhaps not the least important, with regard to the rational promise it holds out of public as well as private benefit. The prodigious extent of sea-coast, which naturally belongs to our island, seems to call the attention of its inhabitants very forcibly to the subject of its fisheries: a subject full of interest, as pointing out to them a never-failing source, not only of subsistence and comfort, but of national wealth.

When we reflect on the amazing riches of the ocean, producing fish in such abundance as that even large draughts of them seem to cause no diminution in the supply, but that, in consequence of their continual migrations, successive shoals will be found day after day, occupying nearly the same situations, we are ready to exclaim, Surely these are the *peculiar* blessings of Providence! It is supposed, indeed, that the increase of fish is incalculably greater than that of any other living creatures; since many sorts, upon a moderate computation, multiply at the rate of a thousand to one. But in vain are these bountiful gifts of Providence bestowed upon us! in vain is the sea stored with food for the subsistence of man! One fettering condition alone, which falls with peculiar hardship on the labour of the people employed in our fisheries, serves to deprive us of the principal advantages which we might naturally promise to ourselves from the possession of so rich and inexhaustible a treasure! This condition arises from the DUTIES ON SALT. Notwithstanding the great benefits derivable from the employment of fishing, the success attending it is often defeated by these impolitic duties. It frequently happens, for instance, that fishing-boats, after taking a cargo of fish, are prevented by contrary winds or calms from reaching a place of sale while the fish is fresh and good : under such circumstances, were the men allowed to *sprinkle* it with a little salt, it might be preserved sweet for a week or two ; being debarred however from this by the salt laws, it is not unusual for them, after the toil and labour of many days, to throw their valuable cargoes overboard. Nor is their own loss the only one sustained on such occasions, thousands of hungry people are thus deprived of a wholesome and plentiful sustenance, which they might otherwise have obtained.

The duties payable on salt are more than thirty times its original value ; and this amounts, in the case of applying it to the preservation of fish, to a prohibition. There is, however, a nominal exemption from these duties in the curing of fish ; but the excise laws, through which they are collected, are so vexatious and ruinous, that few people are found willing to render themselves liable even to an inadvertent breach of them.* It is evident, therefore, that this native source of individual and public wealth, viz. our fisheries, is in a great measure rendered unavailing to us. Nor do we seem able, at the first view, to account satisfactorily for the existence of a tax which bears so hard on the industry, spirit, and energy of the labouring classes, and which must also necessarily tend to abridge the comforts of people of every rank. But when it is understood that these duties produce a MILLION AND A HALF sterling per annum to the Government, the secret of their origin and of the supposed necessity for their continuance stands revealed to us.

A noble attempt was made a few years since, by a man whose life had been devoted to the cause of humanity, to excite the attention of the public to the consideration of our Salt Laws, with a view to their repeal : but though Sir THOMAS BERNARD succeeded so far, as to have been instrumental in bringing this interesting subject under the notice of Parliament, it does not appear that any further public benefit was derived from his unremitted philanthrophic exertions.

It may not be unprofitable to pursue this subject a little further, for the benefit of those who have not read Sir THOS. BERNARD'S interesting publication, entitled, " Case of the Salt Duties." We learn from this, that in February, 1817, Mr. CALCRAFT gave notice in the House of Commons, of a motion for a Committee to take the

---

* An instance occurred in Cornwall, of a person having a quantity of duty-free salt under bond in his cellar near the sea-side, when the tide, which had risen to an unusual hight, washed away a great part of it : in this case, the proprietor was obliged to submit to the severity of the law, the same as though the salt had been fraudulently removed!

laws relative to the trade in salt into consideration: on the day appointed, his motion was negatived by a small majority. In the ensuing session, Mr. CALCRAFT was more successful: a committee was appointed, who went into a full examination of the business, which occupied their attention for the space of several months. The inquiry terminated, however, not more favourably than it had begun; for, though there was not perhaps an individual member of the Committee who was not convinced of the highly injurious tendency of the salt duties to the public welfare, yet as they brought in a *million and a half* annually to the Revenue, Government was not disposed to concede so large a sum, without the equivalent of a commutation tax. The friends of the repeal not being provided with the means of offering efficient taxes to the required amount, their benevolent attempt failed.

Concerning the effects of the salt duties on our fisheries, Sir Thomas Bernard observes, " That our national and individual loss by the existence of the salt duties is very great ; and that *bounties, drawbacks,* and *allowances,* have all proved ineffectual to diminish, in any degree, the amount of that public loss: that, with the greatest local and natural advantages of *any nation on earth,* we allow Holland, America, and other rival States, to *use our salt and our fishing-banks, and afterwards to supplant us in our trade:* that our poor on the sea-coast are robbed of their employment and subsistence, and in the interior, of nutritious and palatable food : our navy is deprived of a valuable nursery for seamen, and of the means of supporting and retaining them in time of peace—and all for the sake of a petty and pitiful income, forced from the *salt proprietor, against every principle of equity and justice.*" [Case of the Salt Duties, p. 34.] He describes also the injurious effects of the salt duties upon our trade and manufactures in a clear and convincing manner: we may follow him in his enumeration of the more important of these.

Salt enters as a necessary ingredient, first, into MINERAL ALKALI or SODA, of which immense quantities would be used in the making of *soap,* and in various other processes, if salt were free of duty. At present we import for this purpose many tons of *barilla,* annually, from Spain, whilst a superior article might be made by us for a little more than half of what it now costs. He estimates (on the authority of Mr. PARKES, an experienced chymist,) that *ten thousand tons* of this would be used in Great-Britain, as soon as the process could be established; which consumption would probably increase in a short time, and it would finally become a valuable branch of our export trade.

Salt might be made, by various chymical processes, to supersede the use of foreign *potash, pearlash,* and *muriatic acid;* which are severally applied to bleaching, calico-printing, dyeing, &c.; and in the preparing of which, great numbers of our poor might be usefully and profitably employed. It might be used also in making *phospate of soda*, for the purpose of fluxing and soldering metals, instead of *borax*, a dear and foreign article.

Sal ammoniac, and many other valuable chymical compositions, may be produced from English salt.

Salt might be used with great advantage in our iron-works, for rendering British bar iron malleable, and for making steel, so as entirely to supersede the necessity of importing the more costly kinds of iron from Russia or Sweden.

Salt is not only thus far necessary to iron-founders, but it is also used as an ingredient in making metallic cements; it is necessary to whitesmiths and cutlers in the operation of case-hardening, and in the process of tempering files and edge-tools. In the refining of silver, too, the reduction of metallic ores, the assaying of metals, and many other processes, salt is constantly used whenever the duties on it do not amount to a prohibition.

Salt is a necessary ingredient in the manufacture of morocco and other kinds of leather, of which a great deal is prepared in England: it is also used in making glass, and in the glazing of earthenware. Owing to the excessive duties on salt, however, *oxide of lead* is mostly substituted for it in our potteries, though highly poisonous; the consequence is, that the health of the persons employed in this part of the pottery business is greatly affected: besides which, the fatal effects of the lead are often felt in families, in the use of earthenware, without their being aware of the cause. This metal is easily dissolved by acids, in culinary uses, and the insidious poison thus received into the stomach has in many instances proved fatal.

Sir THOMAS BERNARD has also clearly shewn the numerous benefits which agriculture would derive from the free and unrestrained use of salt, in a variety of ways. He states that "it contributes not only to the health of cattle and sheep, but accelerates their fattening, and promotes and improves the milk of cows. It prevents the rot in sheep, and the effect of *hoving*, when stock are fed on turnip and clover. Salt renders damaged hay palatable and nutritious; and, if applied in rainy seasons, prevents an undue fermentation and heat in the stack From my experience of its salutary effects on cattle (says Mr. CURWEN), I should consider the free use of it, as a *condiment*, to be the greatest boon Government could bestow on the husbandman."* Since Sir T. BERNARD published his " Case of the Salt Duties," *Rock Salt* has been allowed by law, for the purposes of agriculture, on application being made to the officers of Excise; to whom the purposes for which

---

* Case of the Slt Duties, p. 94.

it is intended must be specified, and a certificate given upon oath of its due application.

This privilege, however, still fettered as it is by the severities of the Excise laws, seems to be but little used by farmers generally; who, in many cases, would rather forego an advantage, than subject themselves to vexatious laws, which they do not understand.

In taking a review of the injurious effects of the salt duties on the general comforts of society, but more especially on those of the poor,—on the *fisheries, trade, commerce, manufactures,* and *agriculture* of this nation, which might be rendered incalculably greater sources of *employment* and *profit* than they now are by the free use of salt, we cannot but deplore the continuance of a tax so vexatious, oppressive, and impolitic. We heartily wish that Government were sufficiently sensible of the general mischief and loss which it occasions to the community at large, and that some remedy or substitute could be found, if only a temporary one, by which a fair trial might at least be made, of the proposed advantages to be derived from a commutation so necessary to the employment and subsistence of our starving poor.

Sir THOS. BERNARD calculates that the poor, whose food consists chiefly of potatoes, pay at the rate of 15 to 1 more than the rich, for the salt they make use of, supposing the number of individuals in their families to be the same.

What an oppressive tax this, on an article of the first necessity to human subsistence; and with which Providence has so bountifully supplied our island by means of salt springs and mines, besides what might be extracted from the briny ocean by which it is surrounded! A tax cruelly exacted from those who are the least able to bear it.

Employment, as applicable to Work-Houses, Prisons, &c.

NUMEROUS have been the contrivances for the abridgment of human labour, and the facilitating of business, which have of late years been introduced into our manufactories, as well as into agriculture. But, however creditable to the ingenuity of man such inventions may be, the real benefits or the actual disadvantages accruing to society from them, must be determined by the effects they produce on the condition of the labouring classes of the people. It would be a truly noble application of the inventive faculties of man, were they directed to the promotion of industry, and to the securing of comfort and a sufficiency of pay to the labourer; more especially in times like the present, when the usual sources of labour are suspended, and in many instances cut off, by an excess of mechanical invention. Nor is it less the interest and duty of good governments, than it is honourable to the friends of humanity, to supply the great mass of the people with useful and constant employment; as, without it, they are apt to become discontented, vicious, and dangerous to the state.

It is not necessary that such employment should be absolutely and immediately productive of pecuniary profit; the *moral* benefits of labour are of infinitely greater importance. Our paupers and criminals must, according to law, be maintained by the state; and therefore it becomes a matter of expediency that they should be employed *at any rate*, whether any immediate gain be derived from their labour or not; nay, even if in some instances it be attended with loss, rather than that those who are able to work should remain idle. Under these impressions, it is pleasing to be able to record a *newly devised means* of useful and healthy employment, which we trust will constitute an era in our agricultural history, at the same time that it promotes the increase of our manufactures. The cultivation of FLAX seems indeed a desirable expedient for the purpose of extending and improving our internal resources as a nation. But considerable prejudices formerly existed with regard to this branch of agriculture. It was supposed, in the first place, that strong or rich soil was necessary to the due and perfect growth of Flax; and, secondly, that the local convenience of large ponds or pits, for steeping it in water during several weeks, was requisite; together with a considerable degree of skill in the subsequent management of it. In consequence, Flax was cultivated only in a few counties or districts. But, by a recent invention, the process of *pitting* or *dew-retting*, which was, besides its inconvenience, exceedingly nauseous and offensive, as well as unhealthy, is found to be unnecessary. It now appears that Flax will grow in ordinary soil, manured as for other crops; that when the seed is ripe (or before it attains that state, if the crop is designed for the finest linen), the flax is pulled up by the roots, and laid on the ground to dry: nor is any extraordinary care or attention required in the harvesting or future management of it.

To prepare Flax for the manufacturer, various ingenious contrivances had been, within the last few years, offered to the public, for which patents were obtained, and which had been more or less successful. The instrument, however, which appears at present the best calculated to answer the desired end is called a "DECORTICATOR," invented by J. LOWDER, esq; of Bath, and for which he has obtained a patent. This instrument bruises the stem or woody part of the plant in such a manner as to separate and detach the harle or fibre from the boon or pith, which last is alone available for the manufacture of linen. Thus, an employment of a desirable kind, applicable either to workhouses, prisons, penitentiaries, or cottages, may be provided with comparative ease by those who have the management of the poor. Nor is it necessary that, wherever the flax is thus prepared, the subsequent stages of manufacturing it into linen should be completed in the same place, for the flax in this state is at all times marketable.

The "Decorticator" is described by a recent writer* as being "very cheap, very portable, of the easiest movement, and simplest construction; it occupies little room, not more than that of a cottage stool, may be worked by any individual, and renders available for manufacture *all* the fibre contained in the plant."

It may not be unnecessary to mention the *manner* in which the "Decorticator" is applied: In the preparatory factory in Bath, the business is effected chiefly by boys of from 8 to 12 years of age. Of course, it is obvious, the same work may be done by adults of either sex, and of almost any age. Children may work alternately on the Decorticator and at other processes of the preparation, if the former should produce considerable fatigue.

The invention of this instrument has already had the effect of producing experimental attempts at the cultivation of Flax in various parts of England, by which some valuable information has been obtained. It is observed, by the writer of the pamphlet before referred to, that flax succeeds well on lands hitherto considered waste; and that, "were grants of such *lands* made to parishes

---

* See "Observations on the means of deriving from Flax and Hemp, Manual Employment for labourers of every age."—Printed and sold by Woolmer, Exeter; Longman, Hurst, Rees, Orme, and Brown, and J. Richardson, Cornhill, London.

by the Crown or by Corporate bodies," and "the vacant hours of our peasantry, and the misspent time of our criminals and paupers, thus beneficially employed, a firm step would be made towards political independence, resting on the industry of a hardy and contented peasantry."* When the philanthropist, indeed, considers the amazing extent of uncultivated land in the United Kingdom (said to be estimated at from 15 to 25 millions of acres†), he will probably hail with peculiar delight, and recommend with peculiar ardour, a means so well calculated as is the cultivation of flax for the renovation and extension of our agricultural prosperity. His view seems to open, too, upon that wonderful and beautiful variety in the appointments of Providence, by which not a fragment of soil was, perhaps, intended to be lost to man, in the whole extent of creation. Thus, after we have appropriated the richer tracts of our country to the raising of *food*, we have it in our power to turn the remaining and more sterile tracts to the production of *clothing*. And this is also agreeable to that general law of our being, by which the soil was not only given to man for cultivation, but was to constitute the principal object of his industry and skill. But, in addition to the beauty and expediency of the plan, we have strong and urgent motives for attempting every thing which is practicable, in order to supply the labouring classes with useful, healthy, and permanent employment. This is a desideratum in the present circumstances of the nation, which we should never cease seeking till we have attained to it. The reduction of the poor's rate depends upon it, as well as the virtues and safety of the state; it being well known, that if the great mass of the people be not constantly employed, as well as fed, vice, and disorder, and misery must ensue. Nor must we omit to mention an obvious and additional advantage which will accrue to *society* from the preference of flax to cotton, resulting from its superior strength and durability. The fashion of the times may be in favour of *cotton;* but when it is considered that cotton is and must be altogether a foreign production, and that the landed and manufacturing interests will both obtain ultimate benefit by the extension of our internal resources of national prosperity, it is not too much to expect that fashion, which is proverbially fickle, may quickly find herself compelled to enlist on the side of reason and common-sense.

Indeed the present time seems peculiarly favourable to the extended culture of those valuable staples, FLAX and HEMP, when our farmers even complain of the superabundant produce of corn, though our stock has not been increased by any importation of foreign corn for a considerable time past.

---

* See "Observations, &c." p. 15.

† Bampfill's First Letter to Sir Thomas Acland, on adapting the Poor Laws to the present state of society.—2d edit. p. 16.

Of that interesting branch of female industry, the *spinning* of Flax, in which women were happily and usefully employed, from the earliest periods of civilized society, we have hitherto said but little, from a knowledge of the overwhelming influence of the "spinning jennies," which have nearly banished from our cottages and the dwellings of our peasants the agreeable and profitable employment of *hand-spinning*.

We are, however, gratified by observing some interesting notices relative to this branch of rural economy in a pamphlet, entitled " A Treatise on the Practical Means of Employing the Poor," by Wm. Salisbury.

This writer observes, "there is a means by which the common spinning-wheel may be substituted for the use of the cottager's family, by a small machine calculated to spin six threads at one time, and give the poor an opportunity of once more reviving that art which was practised, with so much zeal, a century since; and I look forward with great hope, that whenever the culture of Flax and Hemp shall be sufficiently introduced into Great-Britain to supply our own markets, this appendage to female industry will be the means of restoring our poor to a comparative state of independence, and to the consequent exercise of morality; which, with all its attendant virtues, shall become the true characteristic of the British peasant."—The public are much indebted to this philanthropist for the zeal which he has evinced in endeavouring to promote useful employment among the labouring classes, by instituting " A School of Economy" for instructing the poor in various kinds of productive labour. The benevolent reader is respectfully referred to W. Salisbury's pamphlet.

IRELAND has long been famous for its excellent linen. The culture as well as the manufacture of flax is said to be carried on chiefly in the province of Ulster; and there, even among the small farmers or peasants, many of whom go through all the stages of the business, from raising the flax (which they sometimes do on very small plots of ground), to the making of it into linen. These peasants are weavers too; and as soon as they have gathered in their crop of flax, they proceed to steep and dew-ret it, and afterwards dress and prepare it for spinning: the latter is done by females in almost every cottage. When the thread is woven into linen, each man carries his piece to the linen-market, where it is purchased by the *bleacher*.

Flax is also partially cultivated and manufactured in several other districts in Ireland. Benevolent persons in the towns and cities promote this object, as a means of employing the poor; for the spinning of flax is considered in the light of a necessary acquirement among females of the lower classes generally. And it is gratifying to learn that the spinning of thread by *machinery* is but little known in that country.

We understand that it is common, too, for persons not concerned in trade, in Ireland, to have flax manufactured into linen for their own private consumption. In this there is no difficulty, as persons are easily found in most of the counties, who undertake to weave and to finish the linen off fit for use.

We wish nothing better for our own country, than that similar means of agreeable and useful employment could be furnished amongst us.

At all events, it is natural to suppose that Government, as well as the public at large, must be convinced of the necessity of speedily adopting some prompt and effectual measures for the general employment of our numerous and starving poor.

However, we have yet to mention several modes of employment adapted to situations where large numbers of persons are necessarily collected.

For Prisons.—The following kinds come recommended by the benevolent Committee of the " Society for the Improvement of Prison Discipline," &c.* as employments which may be carried on in those receptacles of the vicious, under proper regulations:

" Grinding corn, and dressing flour, malt, &c. by the discipline mill, as well as by hand-mills.

Raising water by the discipline mill or by windlass.

The preparation and dressing of flax, hemp, hair, and wool.

Weaving various articles of clothing for prisons.

Weaving rugs, bed-sacking, and carpeting.

Making rope mats, and fishing and all other kinds of nets.

Tailor, shoemaker, comb, button, pin, and needle maker.

Bookbinder, letter-press printer, engraver, and pencil-maker.

Clock and watch maker, watch-case maker and gilder; and grinding and polishing glasses for watches, spectacles, &c.

Toy-maker, carver and turner of wood, ivory, and brass, and glass bead-maker.

Joiner, cabinet-maker, sieve and measure maker; brush, basket, spinning-wheel, patten, and last maker.

Leather trunks and cases, bellows, whip, and harness maker.

Grinding of drugs and colours, for painters and paper-stainers, by hand-mill.

Grinding and pounding of plaister, lime, stone, shells, glass, &c. for cement.\

Cutting wood and stone, polishing marble, cutting corks, and various kinds of wooden pegs, and tile pins.

Whitewashing, painting, &c. about the prison buildings.

---

* Report, page 109.

FOR FEMALE PRISONEES.

Making wearing-apparel for the prisoners.
Washing, ironing, and mending for prison service.
Knitting and needlework of all kinds.
Weaving sundry articles of wearing-apparel.
Picking, carding, spinning, and winding cotton, wool, silk, flax, or hemp.
Making of women's and children's shoes and gloves.
Platting straw and willow, and making hats for prisoners.
Making stays, braces, fringe, trimming, ribbons, lace, &c."*

[In addition to the foregoing modes of employment suggested in the "Report," the writer of these pages is desirous of impressing on the attention of managers of prisons, workhouses, &c. a very useful process already treated of at page 57 of this work, viz. the Pounding of Oyster-Shells for Manure, which has been carried on successfully in the parish of St. Martin, in London, and by the Society for the Suppression of Mendicity in Dublin.]

The numerous benefits to society (including the reformation of offenders) to be effected by useful employment are too obvious to need to be insisted on. The Committee, in the Report to which we have been alluding, state various instances of them which have occurred in England, as well as in America. We think the following account deserves to be presented to the reader, being part of the "Report of the VISITING JUSTICES upon the state of the Gaol and Bridewell for the County of HANTS:"

"The visiting Justices have the greatest satisfaction in stating, that the corn-mill continues to answer all the purposes for which it was constructed; and that the new mill, ordered to be erected, is now ready, and in actual use. The prisoners have been kept in actual employment during the whole of the last quarter: and although a considerable number of them have been engaged upon the buildings, which after a short time must cease, yet the two corn-mills, with the addition of such handicraft work as has been and may be introduced for the occupation of those who may be incapable of hard labour, will afford ample employment for all the male prisoners that this gaol will contain; and not a single individual will be left, as heretofore, in a state of idleness.

---

* The whole process of converting wool into cloth is carried on at ILCHESTER gaol. All the prisoners are clothed in a dress, every article of which they manufacture; viz. worsted caps, dowlas shirts, jackets, waistcoats, breeches, stockings, and shoes; also beds, mattresses, sheets, linen, &c. for the general use of the prison. The females are employed in making all the prisoners' dresses, and in washing the weekly changes of linen, bedding, &c. A considerable part of the gaol was built entirely by prisoners, and furnished employment to them as masons, bricklayers, carpenters, and painters.

" The good effect anticipated from the introduction of labour, has already manifested itself, in the diminution of refractory husbandry servants committed to this prison; and of vagrants also, since the adoption of a most salutary regulation with respect to them. Both of these descriptions of persons, and particularly the former, have, it is believed, been deterred from the commission of offences, by the dread of compulsory and unprofitable hard labour, upon a restricted diet. Should this alarm continue to operate on the minds of these persons, as the visiting Justices have little doubt but it will, the introduction of labour into this prison will not only have a beneficial tendency in reforming the individuals who may be committed, but occasion the suppression of crime; and consequently diminish the public expenditure: for it was notorious, that before the corn-mill was in actual operation, and the severity of the labour known to the two descriptions of persons before mentioned, so far from reluctance being felt by either, at being committed to gaol, that the one was indifferent about it, and the other not unfrequently sought an asylum within the walls of the prison, where they were comfortably lodged and fed without the infliction of any kind of punishment: but being now kept to hard labour, and prohibited from receiving any assistance from their friends, the treatment is no longer an object of unconcern to the one, or of comfort to the other. The expense to the county, for the vagrants only, has, during one quarter of a year, amounted to no less a sum than 80*l*. 16*s*. 9*d*.; and if the system of reform introduced into the Bridewell should be productive of no other beneficial consequence than to deter many farming servants and vagrants from entering the prison, it will have already effected a great moral and economical advantage. But the *moral* good likely to result from a continuance of the present system *is scarcely to be limited;* and although *profit* has never constituted any part of the object contemplated by the magistrates who projected and have carried the plan into execution, yet the visiting justices think it right to mention, that the clear gain from the labour of the prisoners at the mill, and by baking, amounts, up to the present time, to upwards of 100*l*. It is deserving of notice also that the work performed by the prisoners, in building the addition to the prison, would, if executed by hired mechanics and workmen, have amounted to a very considerable sum."—*Report*, page 34.

The following extracts from this interesting Report of the Committee of the " Society for the Improvement of Prison Discipline" all prove the benefits that have resulted from *labour* in Prisons:

BURY GAOL.—" The Discipline Mill, which has recently been erected at Bury gaol, is capable of grinding wheat and dressing flour with any number of hands, from 16 to 30 at one time. It will grind and dress from 20 to 30 quarters of wheat per week, at 10 hours each day. The machinery consists of two pair of stones, each capable of grinding four bushels per hour; one dressing-mill, which dresses two sacks of flour per hour; and one pair of malt-rollers, which grind 12 bushels per hour; besides hoisting tackle and every other appendage to a complete mill. The total cost of machinery, and fixing ditto, for this establishment was 600*l*. The mill has been at work upwards of three months, to the entire satisfaction of a numerous magistracy, to the great dislike of the prisoners, and to the profit of the county. They keep a regular miller, and grind for hire all corn sent to them for that purpose; and if work of that kind fall short, the governer buys a sufficient quantity of wheat, which is made into flour and sold, yielding by that means a certain profit.

"The object of the discipline mill is, the adoption of a kind of hard labour to which every one would have a natural dislike, and yet such as every one could perform without previous instruction; and is founded on the following principle, viz. that of making use of the joint efforts of all the prisoners, as a first moving power to some branch of manufacture suited to the local circumstances of the county in which the prison is situated: for instance, in Suffolk, Norfolk, and Essex, and some other counties which are exclusively agricultural, the manufacture of flour seems the most eligible; whilst in Lancashire, Yorkshire, &c. throwing, twisting, and spinning mills might be worked by the same power; and in other parts, machinery for pumping water, driving lathes, &c. &c. might be set in motion in like manner. The operation of the convicts would be precisely the same as that which is now effected by the ordinary powers of wind, water, steam, or horses, and they would have no concern or connection with the object of the machinery or manufactory, more than any of the above-named agents: for there would be no difficulty in establishing a mill or manufactory near the boundary wall of a prison, through which a single shaft or axle would have to pass, and thus communicate the power."—*Report*, page 20.

WORCESTER COUNTY GAOL.—"The greatest benefit *as to morals and good conduct* appears to have arisen from the constant employment of all the prisoners confined: the whole of the clothing of the prisoners, shoes, bedding, &c. are manufactured in the gaol, under the direction of the visiting magistrate, elected at the Quarter Sessions. Prisoners, before trial, receive half their earnings; after trial, one-sixth. Diet, 1½ lb. of good wheaten bread and a quart of gruel daily.—*Report*, page 45.

SOUTHWELL GAOL.—"The pecuniary advantage arising from the *labour* of the prisoners will appear sufficiently manifest from the printed abstract of the accounts: the profits have increased progressively since the commencement of the undertaking. *Emolument*, however, has always been regarded as a *secondary* object;

since religious and moral principles are the only basis of permanent reformation and substantial happiness. But industrious habits have been encouraged, as the means of securing subordination within the prison, and of maintaining the prisoners in honesty after their discharge. Many have learned trades during their imprisonment, some have transmitted regular contributions for the support of their families, and others have accumulated a sufficiency to settle themselves in business after their discharge."—*Report*, page 52.

AMERICA.—"Considering the great advantage contemplated to result from the penitentiary system, the mere expense is a matter of secondary consideration; yet experience has proved, in NEW JERSEY, PHILADELPHIA, BALTIMORE, and VIRGINIA, that, under prudent direction and good management, *the profits of the labour of the convicts will produce sufficient to pay all the necessary expenses for their support*, &c. I think the best-conducted penitentiary is at *Baltimore.* I visited that prison a few months ago, and was highly gratified in observing the order, cleanliness, regularity, and industry of the prisoners. I never visited any institution that exhibited such a perfect degree of cleanliness, decency, and regularity, throughout its whole concerns, as the Baltimore prison, the effects of which were evidently marked in the countenances and general deportment of the convicts."—*Report*, page 152.

In BAVARIA, the improvements in the management of the House of Correction are calculated even to excite our astonishment. The following account is extracted from the *"Report,"* page 140:

"The House of Correction, so far as regards the regulation of the work, is an example and a powerful argument in favour of *employing* prisoners. There are 720 persons in this house; and last year, after deducting every expense attending the establishment, there was a *net profit* to Government, in the proceeds of manufactured articles, of 32,000 florins; whereas, before, besides the expenses of the keepers, &c. every prisoner cost from 120 to 140 florins per annum. They have a complete manufactory of broad cloth, even superfine of all colours, blue, scarlet, &c. some as high as 14 florins per yard; there are also shoemakers, tailors, &c.

"In a district containing a population of 2,500,000 persons, in 5 years, *two only* have been sentenced to death; and their sentence is not confirmed, so that it may yet be changed into imprisonment."

IMPROVED MANAGEMENT OF THE POOR AT ILMINSTER.

"We cultivate four acres of land for the use of the poor. This gives employment to those who apply for relief from want of work, and serves to detect the indolent. The produce of this field is appropriated to the use of the workhouse, and the surplus is sold to each needy and deserving pauper, somewhat under the market price, which is charged to them instead of their weekly allowance of cash.

The profit arising from the cultivation of this field with potatoes amounted in the first year, 1817, to 13*l.* 8*s.* 4½*d.*; in 1818, to 68*l.* 9*s.* 4*d.*; and in 1819, sown with wheat, to 24*l.* 4*s.* 4*d.*

" Our workhouse, heretofore, was a receptacle for the profligate and idle, until a resolution was formed to build a workshop in the workhouse-yard, and establish a manufactory. These were completed in 1817, at which time 75 paupers were in the house. No material alteration appeared in our expenditure that year, in consequence of the machinery employed in the factory belonging to the governor of the workhouse.

" In 1818 *the parishioners agreed to purchase the machinery.* As soon as the paupers were acquainted with this determination, they gradually left the house, saying they would work for themselves and not for the parish. In August, 1819, only 38 paupers remained in the house! This reduction arose solely from the paupers being obliged to work a limited number of hours each day. Formerly the expenditure for the house alone was from 60*l.* to 70*l.* 80*l.* and 90*l.* per month; but since Lady-day, 1818, it has not averaged more than 30*l.* per month. This considerable saving is from the reduced number of paupers, who are now obliged to work, if their strength will permit.

"The workshop is 75 feet long and 16 feet wide; the expense of building, about 170*l.* On the ground-floor are two looms, one for weaving dowlass, the other for cloth and serge; conveniences for shearing, wool-combing, &c. On the second floor is the machinery, knitting-school, a place for making and mending shoes, and a store-room, which also serves as a counting-house, and for depositing manufactured articles, &c.

" Wool is purchased sometimes in the fleece (commonly called yoke wool), and at other times in a state ready for combing, as the governor, who is well acquainted with the woollen trade, thinks best: this wool is prepared by the comber, for spinning into worsted of various colours, dyed by the governor. Serges, white and speckled, are wove from the worsted thus properly prepared, for the dresses of the women, and cloth, of a light grey mixture, for the clothing of the men. Stockings are knit for all the paupers in the house, which are stronger, much cheaper, and more comfortable for the winter, than those usually bought at shops; also blankets, sheeting, and dowlass with blue stripes, as a mark of distinction, is wove by the paupers in the house.—Children of *both sexes are taught to knit* as soon as they are capable of holding a needle; and a greater quantity of hose could be sold than is now made. Shoes are also made and repaired, under the immediate inspection of the governor. The out-poor are obliged to pay half towards the expense of clothing, of every description, allowed them (except in cases of extreme poverty, or an indulgence for industry), in order to make them careful of the same. Improvements such as these are practicable in most manufacturing towns. Notwithstanding the long and severe winter of 1820, the slackness of trade, reduction of labour in agriculture, &c. our expenditure was 345*l.* 15*s.* 4*d.* less at Lady-day last than in the preceding year.—*February*, 1821.

Reward Societies.

IN the course of the foregoing chapters, we have endeavoured to promote, as much as it is possible to do by recommendation, the general employment of the poor and labouring classes, as the only rational means of restoring them to that degree of comfort and respectability in society to which they are justly entitled. We cannot, however, deny our conviction, that such is the present abject and degraded state of our poor, occasioned chiefly by the demoralizing effects of the Poor Laws, that the mere *offer* of employment would not, in many cases, be accepted by them as a boon. The labouring classes have been so long accustomed to parish relief (and latterly indeed, very unjustly, in the shape of wages for labour performed), that almost every spark of that independent spirit which their ancestors felt a pride in cherishing, is destroyed; their powers of exertion are palsied, their minds and morals are corrupted and debased, natural affection is extinguished, and the *workhouse* is looked to as the *first* instead of the *last* resort!

Not merely the inmates of workhouses, but the children of the poor generally, are actually trained up to the degrading habits of parish relief, being allowed by the parish-officers to accompany their parents or relatives to the weekly pay-table, or to attend there on their behalf. The discipline which such young persons receive (whilst waiting for several hours together at the door of the workhouse) from the herds of worthless paupers there assembled, gives them an early predilection for the parish pay-table; nor can we wonder that when they grow up, they should determine to resort to the same degrading practice.

It was an error of humanity in many of our pious ancestors, that, in distributing their alms, they regarded the motive rather than the end; not being aware that, in removing the *incitement to industry*, they did more real injury than benefit to the objects of their bounty. In the administering of charity, we should always remember, " that if the manner in which relief is given to the poor is not a *spur to industry*, it becomes, in effect, a *premium to sloth and profligacy.*"

It is now generally admitted that our forefathers were mistaken in the principles and application of charity, and that *we* are paying dear for their errors; not only in having grievous and intolerable burthens entailed upon us, but in feeling that the effects of the pauper system are equally injurious to the poor themselves, as they are to the other classes of society.

As the evils which we now deplore appear to have originated in *mistaken benevolence*, without duly considering that the nature and condition of man require a continual excitement to *labour*, so that each individual should become instrumental in providing for his own wants, we should endeavour to seek for a remedy adapted to the natural state of man.

We should always bear in mind that the human character is made up of a variety of desires and passions, which were designed to fulfil the wise purposes of our beneficent Creator. In our endeavours, therefore, to counteract the vicious and obstinate habits which the continual operation of the poor laws has tended to confirm in the poor and labouring classes, we ought to bring to our aid those elementary passions in man, which, under a wise control, may be made subservient to the happiest purposes.

Most of us are sensible of the powerful principle of SELF-LOVE in our own breasts, not only when we were children, but through the course of our lives. The love of distinction, as arising from this principle, acts as strongly in the breasts of the poor as in those of the rich; and has been observed to excite men to the most surprizing actions. The desire of being distinguished has overcome the fear of death, in numerous instances.

Under these considerations, we respectfully recommend to those who are concerned for the improvement of the moral condition of the labouring poor, to institute, as much possible, REWARD SOCIETIES, for promoting and encouraging habits of industry, sobriety, economy, and every other moral virtue. For though the fear of punishment may deter from atrocious and criminal actions, yet, to produce in the labouring classes a superior line of conduct, to excite them to prudence or exertion beyond the level of mediocrity, and to fix in their minds and hearts good principles and virtuous habits, we ought to have recourse to *rewards, commendation,* and *encouragement.*

Indeed, in the present degraded and demoralized state of the lower classes of society, the higher orders will find that the exercise of disinterested kindness and well-directed encouragement towards their poorer brethren will tend more effectually to produce a reformation in their habits, than any other means. Nothing will so powerfully excite a spirit of virtuous emulation among the poor, as the bestowing of certain marks of distinction by the rich, publicly, and in the face of the country, as well as their granting pecuniary rewards to those individuals who shall have best deserved them.

The value of these premiums would, most probably, be estimated more by the circumstances under which they might be given than by their intrinsic worth: for instance, a silver medal of the value of half a crown, with an appropriate inscription or device, bestowed on a deserving youth, as an acknowledgment of good conduct, would, doubtless, be exhibited and preserved with conscious satisfaction and pride during his life, and be considered with similar feelings of exultation by his son after his decease.

As the impressions made on the mind, during the season of youth, are stronger and more lasting than at any other period of life, we would begin with bestowing marks of distinction upon children, as rewards for their punctual and diligent attendance at school, and for their good conduct therein.

To boys or girls for early proofs of industry, and for the first 5s. saved out of their own earnings, and deposited in a bank for savings. For their regular and orderly attendance at their proper places of public worship, for their exemplary behaviour before other children, and especially for dutiful and affectionate conduct towards their parents and those who may have a claim to their attention.

For their continuance in habits of economy and for their regularly depositing a part of their earnings in some public institution of acknowledged safety.

To young persons as they advance in life, who continue to give proofs of good conduct with regard to industry, sobriety, prudence, and economy.

To such as not only have made it a rule to save part of their earnings until they settle in life, but who prudently determine not to enter into the marriage state *too early*, nor without having first made some provision for the necessary wants of a young family.

To female servants who have maintained a character for prudent and orderly conduct, and for faithful services towards their employers; and who have continued the longest in the same situation ; and have particularly distinguished themselves for plain modest dress, suitable to their station, not having been led away by foolish fashions.

To men servants of farmers, who have served under one master during the greatest number of years, whether living in the house or not, who have maintained good characters, and saved most money from their wages whilst single, some reward is certainly due.

Too much encouragement can scarcely be held out to men of all ages, who have had resolution enough to withstand inducements to the unnecessary visiting of alehouses, and who have not allowed their children even to *enter* the doors of such places. It is obvious that the frequenting of public-houses has proved destructive to the comfort and well-doing of the male sex, in like manner as an excessive fondness for dress and finery has been ruinous to females, as well servants as others, in the lower stations of life.

Pecuniary, and honorary, rewards should both be publicly given to industrious and deserving labourers in husbandry or in manufactures, who have brought up the greatest number of children without parish relief, and supported good moral characters.*

Also to deserving persons of either sex, who have assisted or maintained their aged or infirm parents, or other relatives, by means of their own industry and good conduct.

To cottagers who occupy small plots of ground, whether they are applied to the culture of potatoes or other crops; to the keeping of a pig or a cow; and to those who manage their ground in the best manner, and make it the most productive, in proportion to its extent, some reward should be publicly bestowed.

Cottagers who keep bees, and manage them in the best style, whereby the greatest quantity of honey and wax is produced, are entitled to public reward.

Mothers of families who bring up their children in early habits of order, industry, and cleanliness ; teaching the boys to knit, make nets, and mend their garments, and the girls to spin wool and flax, as well as to sew and knit; or who train up their daughters to be good servants—such mothers deserve to be recompensed, and to be held up to public notice.

As it is probable that, in most cases, there will be gradations of merit in the candidates for rewards, so it appears reasonable that corresponding degrees of value in the prizes bestowed should be observed, from the most deserving down to the least.

Many other subjects of reward may be found worthy of public notice, if this *principle* be recognised, which we trust will be the case. Indeed we entertain a most cheering belief, that, if REWARD SOCIE-TIES were generally established throughout this country, and conducted with kindness and impartiality towards the deserving poor, their beneficial effects would soon be felt and acknowledged.

They would tend to revive that spirit of manly independence which is the characteristic of Englishmen, and which has been so much blunted by our system of poor laws.

Were rewards for industry, sobriety, cleanliness, economy, and other moral virtues, impartially distributed among the poor, by the higher classes, they would have an effect to raise in the former a desire to possess a good name : the satisfaction imparted would teach them the value of those gradations of rank and condition which belong to a well-regulated state of society, whilst it advanced them to a higher scale in the same. It would create a reciprocity of regard and good-will between the rich and the poor, and promote a happy union and community of interest, which is always desirable to a free and virtuous people.

---

* The parish of LUTON, in Bedfordshire, have recorded in their vestry-book the meritorious conduct of *George Wursley*, a labourer of that parish, *who had brought up fifteen children without receiving any assistance, or relief from the parish.* In consequence of meeting with an *accident*, this industrious and deserving man once received from the parish officer *ten shillings,* which, however, he took care to return to the Vestry, with thanks, after his recovery!

Servants.

In a work, the professed object of which is the employment of the lower orders of society and the improvement of their moral condition, it appears not improper to notice the circumstances of servants in relation to their employers, especially as they form so large a proportion of the entire mass of the people.

It is a fact coming within the observation of most persons, that no complaint is more generally heard than that against "bad servants." On a subject, therefore, so universally important, we shall take leave to make a few observations.

If this complaint be founded in truth, it becomes us to inquire into the circumstances which may have occasioned so general a dereliction of moral obligation. The subject naturally forms itself into two divisions, viz. the conduct of servants towards their masters and mistresses, and that of masters and mistresses towards their servants. They have their distinct and somewhat different parts to act; but if either party neglect, in any considerable degree, the performance of those duties which their station assigns to them, moral disorder is produced, by which both are more or less affected.

Servants are commanded, by Scripture authority, to be "obedient to their masters, with fear, and in singleness of heart; not with eye-service as men-pleasers, but as the servants of Christ; with good-will doing service, as to the Lord, and not to men; knowing that whatsoever good thing any man doeth, the same shall he receive of the Lord, whether he be bond or free."

That servants "answer not again:" "not purloining; but that they be subject to their masters, with all fear; not only to the good and gentle, but also to the froward."

And that masters "do the same thing" unto their servants, "forbearing threatening;" and that "they give unto them that which is just and equal; knowing that *their* Master also is in heaven: neither is there any respect of persons with him."

Employers can no more do without servants than servants can do without employers: this reciprocity of interest and duty clearly points out the advantage which would ensue from their mutually consulting the welfare and comfort of each other, remembering the *golden rule*, to "do as they would be done unto." "Whatsoever ye would that men should do to you, do ye even so unto them."

Some masters and mistresses are petulant, hasty, proud, choleric, impatient, and easily provoked; whilst some servants are pert, insolent, disobedient, and perverse: to bear with such failings, does indeed require the exercise of no ordinary share of Christian virtue on either side.

But, supposing the temper and behaviour of both parties to be those of mediocrity, such as may be borne with under a moderate exercise of prudence and self-command, nothing will conduce so effectually to mutual comfort and happiness, as for each to endeavour to be, in all things, kind and benevolent towards the other.

It is a common observation, that "*good* masters make *good* servants:" and it is honourable to *both parties* when they have lived a great number of years together; a circumstance which generally produces lasting esteem and regard on both sides.* This however is, unhappily, not the case when masters or mistresses give way to angry and vehement tempers, abusing their servants for trivial faults, and sometimes on account of groundless suspicions. When such conduct becomes habitual, it soon sours the temper of servants, nor will good ones remain long in families where they meet with treatment of this sort.

Frequent or hasty changes are equally unfavourable to the interests of masters and mistresses as to those of servants. The former, when they are known to part with their servants on slight grounds, seldom have good ones offer service to them; whilst the latter, from their unsettled habits and frequent changes, are generally poor, and sometimes destitute.

Servants, especially, should endeavour to submit patiently to circumstances, which, though unpleasant, may ultimately be for their good; and employers will derive satisfaction from being condescending towards their servants, and making allowance for faults not originating in wilfulness or perverseness.

When it is found necessary, however, to dismiss a servant, it should be done, if possible, in a Christian temper, and not with wrath or passion. There are few offences that will justify the dismission of a servant *suddenly*, or late at night; especially if the party be a female, and have not friends by whom she may be immediately accommodated with lodging. Should a servant, in such a case, fall into snares or temptations, and swerve from the path of virtue, great indeed must be the responsibility of those who may have driven her into a situation so exposed and dangerous.

---

* Here the writer desires to pay a tribute of merited regard to the memory of a faithful servant, who lived with him 22 years; during which period she performed the entire work of the house, with credit and satisfaction. With a disposition submissive and kind, she united every good quality of a servant. Her conduct was prudent and exemplary. She dressed in a manner becoming her station—plain, decent, and frugal; and spent nothing idly or unnecessarily. Her savings (with interest arising) exceeded £100, which she wisely intended as a provision for age or infirmities. And had she survived her master, this worthy domestic would have received from him an annuity for her life, sufficient to have made her latter days comfortable.

The importance of servants to the welfare and happiness of society ought to be well considered—that they are necessarily the nurses and companions of our children during their tender years; that they have the care of our property; and (if good ones) are instrumental to many of our comforts through the whole course of our lives. These considerations should lead us to make some allowances for the local circumstances which tended to form their manners and dispositions, and to pay some necessary attention to the cultivation of good habits in them.

It is well known that servants are usually selected from that class of persons a little above the lowest, whose education, as affected by the instilling of moral and virtuous principles, is, not unfrequently, but too little attended to. The examples of their parents, and of the associates of their younger years, are far from being instructive or favourable to virtue; whilst the bad habits they contract in the streets with idle comrades are so powerful as scarcely ever to be eradicated. With such a ground-work, therefore, it cannot excite wonder, that, when these young persons are received into our families as servants, they should prove untractable, and often conduct themselves in a very unsatisfactory manner, and especially when they are suddenly placed in situations where several servants are kept: by being too well fed, and not having perhaps sufficient employment, it is to be expected that such a change will produce levity, giddiness, and imprudence, in minds little capable of resisting temptation.

From scanty fare at home, when these young persons are received into families, where they get plenty of food, and better clothing and lodging than they had ever before been accustomed to, with perhaps too little work to perform, the very circumstances of such repletion and ease are enough to indispose them to their duty, independently of their former bad habits, or of the worse examples in the way of which they may now be thrown.

But, were masters and mistresses to consider sufficiently their moral responsibility as heads of families, and their duty as guardians and conservators of their servants, they would give them good counsel, and set them good examples also: they would instruct them in their moral and religious duties, and train them to habits of virtue and piety; endeavouring to provide them with suitable exercise for their minds, when they have not full employment for their bodies. If this were happily the case, both parties would become more attached to each other: masters and mistresses would be more sensible of the value of good servants, and not be disposed to part with them for trivial causes; nor would servants then be so fond of novelty and change as they now too generally are.

It may be observed in this place, that most of the vices and errors of female servants have been found to originate in an excessive fondness for dress and finery. This propensity leads them to exact high wages from their employers. And when high wages do not prove sufficient to gratify their follies, they have sometimes had recourse to theft and prostitution, and at length have not scrupled to break through all moral restraint, and to violate all laws human and divine.

Probably these young and inexperienced females had not received that salutary check to such a propensity which their employers might have given, by counsel and admonition, so as to prevent the growth of their desires: many mistresses, on the contrary, encourage their servants in these follies; whereas, if they had set them good examples, and advised them to wear such clothes only as are suitable to their station, plain, modest, and substantial; nay, even if employers were to make it a condition, on hiring their servants, that they should not exceed a certain sum in clothing, and deposit a part of their wages regularly every year in a Bank for Savings; these precautions would, in many instances, be attended with the happiest moral results.

A great *desideratum* in society, particularly in large cities and towns, is a *proper* medium of communication for families wanting servants, as well as for servants wanting places. At present this communication is too often undertaken by persons not possessing the best principles, who open what they call "REGISTER OFFICES for Servants," in applying to whom, a fee is required to be paid on taking down the name of the applicant, and another when the object is attained. To these Offices few servants of unexceptionable character apply; nor do families of the first repute often have recourse to them, except in cases of emergency.

The principal applicants to such Offices are raw and inexperienced females, who having long waited, in vain, for situations, and perhaps spent all their money or pawned most of their clothes for lodging and sustenance, are at length induced to accept of service in disorderly houses, to which they are thus recommended.

To guard against such mischief, and to promote as much as possible virtuous behaviour and the accommodation of families, it is highly desirable that in all large towns and cities REGISTRY OFFICES, for servants of *good character only*, should be opened, and conducted by committees of respectable females, who might be able to bestow a portion of their time upon undertakings on which the welfare of society appears so greatly to depend.

A Registry Office of this description has been managed by a few benevolent ladies in BATH during the last two years, and has been productive of very satisfactory results; and a similar one, except that it is upon a much more extensive scale, and embraces the principle of *encouraging,* by rewards, good servants who have continued stationary several years in the same service, as well as that of accommodating them with situations, has happily been in operation during a much longer period in *Hatton-Street,* LONDON. A Society for encouraging and rewarding good servants has also been established at Manchester, and been productive of results equally gratifying.

We beg strongly to recommend to the serious and earnest attention of heads of families, if they desire to effect a salutary reformation among servants, a plan that has been attended with the best effects at CHELTENHAM; namely, the instituting of Schools of Industry for training girls as *servants of all work,* of which some account is already given in page 11.

When we consider the uncultivated soil from which servant girls, in general, are taken; the ignorance in which they are brought up; the contamination to which they are liable, during their youth, from bad examples set them by their parents, and their street associates; and the very little of any thing good which they can possibly learn at home; we think the sooner they are rescued from such scenes of ignorance and vice, and placed where they may be exercised in plain, useful, and virtuous habits, to fit them for *under servants,* the better for themselves and for society in general.

Upon the whole, we are of opinion that, however general or well founded the complaint against "bad servants" may be, there is no probability of much amendment being effected in this province of the community until masters and mistresses first determine *to do their duty.* Let *them* begin with setting good examples, and giving good counsel, to their servants; let *them* be kind and considerate towards them, not requiring more of them than what is just and equal, but place themselves, as it were, in their situations, whereby they would be better able to judge of the feelings of servants when hardly dealt by. And, lastly, let them endeavour to promote the moral and temporal welfare of their servants, as members of the same common family, for whose redemption, as well as their own, the same Saviour died.

Nothing would tend more effectually to produce a reformation so highly desirable, than for mothers to bring up their daughters, generally, to the knowledge of domestic affairs, and to the performance of the duties required of them as heads of familes, instead of making them devote so much of the season of youth to mere exterior accomplishments.

The subject is indeed copious as well as interesting, and much more might be said than our limits will admit of; but we shall be content to conclude this article by presenting the reader with a few extracts from a work entitled "Hints and Observations seriously addressed to Heads of Families, in reference chiefly to female domestic Servants; by HENRY GEO. WATKINS, M.A." We cannot too highly applaud the unremitted exertions of the pious writer in laying down regulations on this important subject; nor too much admire the beneficial effects of his labour of love, in various ways, for the improvement and encouragement of female Servants.

On the government of a family this experienced writer observes, "Though there are many, very many honourable exceptions, yet it would be saying too much to assert that ALL who may have occasion to employ servants *have a sufficient government of their temper*, or are so fully acquainted as might be wished with the duties required for a moral purveyance of a household ; or possess minds sufficiently discriminating to appreciate well-intentioned services, to distinguish between duplicity and integrity, and to *make reasonable and Christian allowance for the failings of their fellow-creatures." Preface*, page 5.

AUTHORITY.—"A mild government the best maintains its authority. Ferocity obtains only temporary obedience. Authority is influence and power. These are talents of great worth, weapons that are not to be cast away, but nevertheless used with judgment. A real Christian mistress will steadily maintain her authority, that she may have due influence over her domestics; but she will not do it by a proud and assuming deportment. She will endeavour to be the mother as well as the mistress of the family. By entering, as occasion requires, into the feelings and trials of her servants, she will shew that her *superiority* is for their *comfort* and advantage ; and that she can befriend them in various ways, in which their equals could not do it. Her daily conduct will be the result of such considerations as these : ' What have I that I have not received ?' ' The Lord maketh poor, and maketh rich ;' ' he setteth up one, and putteth down another.' ' The same Providence which has appointed me to govern, might have ordained that I should have been the servant ; and therefore I will walk in my house with a sincere and upright mind and conduct.' Some, now very respectable heads of families, are the children of parents that were once servants, and they are indebted to GOD alone that they themselves are not so. On the other hand, many that have borne high authority in families, have sunk in society below the level of honest and comfortable servitude !" *Hints &c.* page 24.

"It therefore behoves heads of families most especially to aim at ruling *in the fear of God ;* that is, to conduct themslves with Christian kindness to their inferiors, with some consideration for their perhaps friendless state; with forbearance as to their minor faults, and with strict justice in every thing. As it would not be fit that they should enter into argument with us, or introduce another to plead their cause, as is in most other cases allowed ; and as, in pleading their own, they may be liable, without evil intent, to the charge of petulancy or insolence: let us take care, in words and deeds, to give them that which is just and equal, knowing that we have also a Master in heaven, 'who regardeth the rich no more than the poor, for they are all alike the work of *his* hands.' As every work will be brought into judgment, it will not be among the last or least inquiries which we shall have to answer, whether, through a very mistaken selfishness, we regarded our servants in the same light as we did our horses, as mere instruments of our own personal convenience or equipage; or, on the other and better hand, whether we viewed those under our authority as placed there by the providence of GOD, not only for our good, but for *theirs* also. A master and mistress are as much appointed of GOD to be his ministers for good to their servants, as far as their greatest influence and most persevering endeavours will go, as parents are required to bring up their children in the nurture and admonition of the Lord. The duties are of course different in some respects, but the responsibility, to GOD the universal Father, is the same!!" *Hints &c.* page 30.*

On promoting the Industry and temporal Comfort of poor Children.

IT has been before attempted, in the course of this work, to impress the reader's mind with the importance of combining early habits of industry with moral and religious instruction in schools for poor children, from a full conviction, that nothing will tend more effectually to promote their temporal comfort than the teaching them, betimes, those methods by which they may obtain an honest livelihood as they advance in life. We are persuaded that it is chiefly because the poor are not so educated, that juvenile depravity has attained its present alarming height.

To educate the poor, in a way that will best qualify them to fill with propriety those stations in which Providence has placed them, ought to be the primary object of the friends of order and humanity. It appears reasonable, therefore, to assert, that the confining the instruction of these persons to mere reading and writing is at best but a partial good; and indeed if this knowledge be not attended with some sense of religion and morality, it commonly becomes an evil instead of a good.

Such being the settled conviction of our mind, we shall add to our former suggestions on this subject the following

---

* The public are also much indebted to the same pious and benevolent author for his "Friendly Hints to Female Servants, for their improvement and encouragement;" also, for his "Sunday School Tracts, or Kitchen Library."

EXTRACT FROM THE REPORT OF THE COMMITTEE OF THE
METHODIST DAY AND SUNDAY SCHOOLS, LIVERPOOL,
FOR THE YEAR, 1820.*

" The lower room is intended to be used as a general work-room, where the boys will be taught to make and mend their own shoes and clothes; and the girls the art of domestic spinning, and such other employment as may be hereafter beneficial to them. By thus uniting useful labour with mental instruction, the committee hope so to bring up the children to habits of early industry, that they will be well prepared to fill up those subordinate situations in society to which they may be called, with credit to themselves, and with advantage to their employers.

" The great utility of such an addition to their establishments was so affectionately urged by a kind and benevolent friend, and accompanied with such liberal offers of assistance, that the committee were induced to make the experiment, as far as it was practicable, with the limited conveniences which they had for the purpose, immediately after the opening of Leeds-street day school. The result has more than answered their most sanguine expectation; for, in the short space of time that has since elapsed, upwards of 100 of the girls in Leeds-street, 40 in Brunswick, and nearly the same number in Jordan-street schools, have learned to spin the common East-India cotton into yarn, which has been knit by the children into upwards of 200 pair of stockings, and 60 petticoats and tippets. Many of the children are now wearing these articles of their own manufacture, as rewards for their diligence and proficiency in learning, and for their general good behaviour; whilst all those who are in the greatest need of clothing, and whose parents are too poor otherwise to obtain them, have the opportunity of purchasing them at the cost price of the materials, which is generally from 3d. to 5d. per pair for good stout stockings, and in proportion for other articles.

" From this early initiation of the children in the art of useful labour, one advantage, which had been anticipated by the promoters of the plan, has already resulted, viz. the production of a corresponding good effect upon the minds of the parents. Many of those, who had never before seen the great advantage of domestic industry, are now anxious to learn from their children, and to introduce into their houses and cellars the almost universally neglected or forgotten arts of DOMESTIC SPINNING and KNITTING. They are now convinced, that a large portion of that time which had been formerly wasted or misemployed may be very advanta-

* Sunday School Teachers' Magazine for April, 1821, page 106.

geously occupied; and, if the means were placed within their reach, they would now gladly improve it.

"In a town like Liverpool, where there is so little employment either for women or their children, it is highly important, and becomes the duty and interest of every wellwisher to his country, to encourage, as much as possible, every indication of a desire to return to those habits of domestic industry once so general among the poor; and which, in consequence of the present very low price of the raw material, may be prosecuted with the greatest advantage. An industrious woman might readily spin two pounds of Bengal cotton in the course of a week, besides attending to her domestic engagements: the yarn would be sufficient to make four large or seven small pairs of stockings, which the children might easily knit after their school-hours in the evenings; and thus, for the sum of 1s. 2d. (the price of the cotton) and the time employed in spinning and knitting, which time would otherwise have been worse than lost, suitable articles of clothing of the value of 7s. or 8s. are obtained. Such are the immediate good effects that may be produced by the system of employment which has been so successfully introduced into the above schools. Should this plan be perseveringly observed in these, and become general in all other such institutions throughout the country, who can calculate the good effects that will hereafter be produced on the moral conduct and general habits of the poor? Is it not reasonable to expect, that, by the adoption of such means as the above, that spirit of independence, or rather of dependence upon themselves and their own exertions for their support, which was formerly at once the characteristic and boast of the labouring classes of society in this country, may be again revived?

"It was with a view of raising them in the scale of society, by exciting those latent principles of independence which it is so desirable to encourage, that, about three years ago, the committee wished to make the experiment of charging each child, in the Brunswick day school, a small weekly sum for the education there received. They began with 1d. per week, and in a very short time they had the satisfaction to find it was productive of the most beneficial effects, both on the feelings and conduct of the children. Several who, previously to this arrangement, appeared to set but little value on the privilege they enjoyed, and evidenced this by their frequent absence from school, no sooner found they must pay something towards the expense of their education, than they became at once more diligent in their attendance and more regardful of the instructions given them; whilst both parents and children were more generally satisfied with an institution, which, by accepting something like a compensation, however small, removed that unpleasant feeling, which even many of the poor have, in receiving a merely gratuitous education. And though the sum of one penny per week may appear too trifling to produce any such effects, yet to many of the parents of these poor children, and particularly those who have several at school, it is certainly an object, and has, in many cases, been the means of reconciling both to a system of discipline with which they were often previously dissatisfied. This plan has since become general throughout all the Methodist schools in this town; the terms now being one penny per week, from those children who are taught to read, and write on slates; and three halfpence per week from those who write in copy-books, and are taught any additional employment. This regulation, with the augmented numbers of children now admitted into the schools, will render important pecuniary help to the committee; who confidenly anticipate that one-fourth of that heavy expenditure, the whole of which they could have hardly hoped to raise from the charities of the public, will be contributed by the children themselves.—Amount received from the children in the last year, £147. 12s. 6d."

We congratulate the benevolent managers of Schools for the Poor at Liverpool on these zealous endeavours to improve the moral and temporal condition of the children under their care; and are convinced that they can scarcely render a greater good to society, than in continuing to use the means which they have so judiciously adopted. To unite early habits of employment with moral and religious instruction, is the best sort of education that can be given to children, whose labour will be the only rational and honest means of their future subsistence. We therefore hope the example alluded to will be followed generally, in schools for the poor, throughout the nation.

The spinning of "coarse Bengal cotton," to be wrought into stockings and other garments for the poor, appears to us somewhat in the light of a new and valuable process, which is capable of being adopted in those of our large commercial towns and cities where manufactories are not generally carried on.

The preparing and manufacturing of our native and valuable staples, WOOL and FLAX, and their importance as affording almost inexhaustible means of employing the poor, are so generally known and allowed, as to make it unnecessary to repeat observations which we have already made on this subject.

But we are particularly desirous of improving every hint that may come to our knowledge, as applicable to "Schools of Industry," and to give every possible encouragement to those light manipulations which may be easily and agreeably performed by children, and which are not likely to become oppressive to them, or prejudicial to their health.

Can any reasonable objection be made to teaching all poor children, males as well as females, to knit and mend stockings?

They are employments that may be resumed in almost any situation, and would profitably fill up a portion of time which might otherwise be mispent.

The making of nets of different kinds may properly be introduced into these schools. Nets may be applied to various purposes (besides catching fish). They would be more generally used in preserving fruit from being destroyed by birds, if they could be readily obtained, and at a cheap rate.

Basket-making appears also to be a fit employment for poor children. Baskets may be wrought of whole or split straw, rushes, osiers, &c. Straw hats and bonnets for the poor, and bee-hives, might be made in these schools.

In all the sorts of employment we have enumerated, we consider the expectation of pecuniary profit as not worthy to be compared with the *moral* benefits that would infallibly result from early habits of industry, which, when once acquired, are seldom relinquished.

These subjects have been already noticed in pages 4, 5, and 6, and elsewhere in this work.

The writer was lately much gratified by visiting the "Military Asylum" at Southampton, where every article of clothing which the boys wear is made up by themselves. This gives them a facility of providing for their wants in all the probable circumstances of their future life. Nor is the good order and diligence of these boys less deserving of admiration, than the proficiency which they evince in the ordinary branches of learning, or their attention to their moral and religious duties.

In the "Military Asylum," the philanthropist sees nothing which he cannot approve, except the practice of training boys to the art of WAR, which Christianity will, nevertheless, sooner or later, put an end to.

In the foregoing pages we have suggested the means which appear to us best calculated to promote virtuous habits and comfort among the labouring classes, and to correct those disorders which exist principally among the lower orders of society. We are convinced, however, that nothing will effectually improve their condition, or overcome that selfish spirit which seeks to aggrandize itself at the expense of others, until we individually endeavour to practise the commandments of our Saviour : "Thou shalt love the Lord thy God with all thy heart, and with all thy soul, and with all thy mind. This is the first and great commandment. And the second is like unto it, *Thou shalt love thy neighbour as thyself.* On these two commandments hang all the law and the prophets."

Were we to write books without number, and propose plans without end, for improving the condition of the poor, they would produce but little benefit, unless this divine principle of *love* were found operating in our hearts. LOVE towards one another, or Christian charity, as it is described in the New Testament, would rectify the disordered state of society, and convert that which now unhappily resembles a wilderness into a fruitful garden.

Pure Christianity would, alone, teach us our social as well as religious duties: it is a principle at once kind, humane, gentle, and commiserating; it inclines those who are actuated by its divine influence to sympathize in the distresses of others, and, as much as lies in their power, to promote the comfort and happiness of all. A good man is a wellwisher, and, when he has the opportunity, a benefactor to his species: one who takes delight in doing good. To such a man the distressed may appeal as to a universal friend.

On Christianity, then, on the practice of those blessed principles which Jesus Christ came into the world to teach by his own example, we must depend for an effectual reformation of the existing disorders of society. Christianity alone will enable us to " love our neighbour as ourselves;" to promote the moral and temporal good of the poor by the means which GOD and nature have appointed, of which *labour* is a chief and indispensable part. Without employment, it is scarcely possible that the poor can be either virtuous or happy. Let them return to their former rational and cheerful occupations of industry in their *own dwellings*, to the various processes of preparing WOOL, FLAX, &c. for the manufacturer, in which the labouring classes have been usefully employed during many centuries, and they will be comparatively happy.

These are no Utopian or visionary schemes, but the result of sober reason and calm observation. Let us have recourse to such means, and society will soon wear a more encouraging appearance: the language of misery and discontent, which now assails us on visiting the abodes of the poor, will be changed into that of cheerful satisfaction as soon as they become the instruments of ministering to their own wants, and *not till then.*

An anonymous writer has beautifully observed, " The time is not far distant, when statesmen and political economists will perceive and acknowledge that the stability of a government, and the strength and happiness of an empire, depend, not upon a numerous, degraded, and half-starved population; but on one in which, from the prevalence of a spirit of virtuous independence, the *necessaries*, if not the comforts of life, are enjoyed by all; and where, from early habits of industry and prudence, the firmest foundation is laid for the superstructure of a highly moral and religious national character."

But this charming description can only be fully realized as Christianity advances in the world, and changes our hearts individually.

TO CONCLUDE, THEN,

We shall present the reader with the following outline of a character, who in the spirit, and according to the example of his divine Master, spent his time in " DOING GOOD."

" COTTON MATHER, D.D. F.R.S., was born at BOSTON, in NEW ENGLAND, in the 17th century.

" He commenced a life of the most active beneficence when very young; and at the age of 16 adopted as a maxim, 'that a power and an opportunity TO DO GOOD not only gives a right to the doing it, but makes it a positive *duty*.' On this maxim he determined to act, and continued to do so during the remainder of his days. Accordingly, he began in his father's family by doing all the good in his power to his brothers and sisters, and to the servants.

" After he had attained to man's estate, he imposed on himself a rule, ' never to enter any company, where it was proper for him to speak, *without endeavouring to be useful in it ;*' dropping, as opportunities might offer, some instructive hint or admonition. By way of improving every moment of his time, he avoided the paying or receiving any unnecessary or impertinent visits: and, to prevent intrusion, he caused to be written in large characters over the door of his study these admonitory words, ' BE SHORT.' Not a day passed without some contrivance on his part ' TO DO GOOD,' nor without his being able to say at the close of it that some part of his income had been distributed for pious purposes.

" He husbanded his time with the greatest exactness, by paying a strict regard to method; and, that all his pursuits might be arranged to the best advantage, he divided his business systematically, by proposing to himself a certain question in the morning of each day, in the following order: *Sabbath morning*—What shall I do as a pastor of a church, and for the good of the flock under my charge? *Monday*—What shall I do for the good of my family? *Tuesday*—What shall I do for my relations abroad? *Wednesday*— What shall I do for the Churches of the LORD, and for the more general interests of religion in the world? *Thursday*—What good may I do in the several societies to which I belong? *Friday*—What special subjects of affliction and objects of compassion may I take under my particular care? and what shall I do for them? *Saturday*—What more have I to do for the interest of GOD, in my own heart and life?

" By this careful observation of method, and a celerity in the despatch of business, he was not only enabled to perform the duties of his pastoral office, as well as the important ones towards GOD and *his neighbour*, but he found time to write a great number of books, of which he published several hundreds.

"Among the writings of this pious man, was a valuable little work, entitled 'ESSAYS TO DO GOOD;' concerning which Dr. FRANKLIN (who also deserves to be ranked among the friends and benefactors of mankind), in a letter to Dr. MATHER, son of the author, *dated from Passy, in France, Nov.* 10, 1779, writes thus: 'When I was a boy, I met with a book, entitled 'Essays to do good,' 'which I think was written by your father. It gave me such a turn 'of thinking as to have had an influence on my conduct through 'life: for I have always set a greater value on a *doer of good* than 'any other kind of reputation; and if I have been, as you seem to 'think, a useful citizen, the public owes the advantage of it to that 'book.'" See *Life of Cotton Mather*.

If it were necessary to prove that this principle of beneficence is capable of exciting men to the most arduous, as well as to the most generous actions, numerous instances might be adduced, of those who have spent their worldly substance in relieving the distresses or promoting the welfare of their fellow beings; who have visited the chambers of sickness, or more loathsome dungeons; who have clothed the naked, fed the hungry, or otherwise ministered to the necessities of the poor. It would be sufficient merely to cite the names of JOHN HOWARD, JONAS HANWAY, and RICHARD REYNOLDS, as those whose good works have established the efficacy of this Christian principle.

To these names deserves to be added that of Sir THOS. BERNARD; a man whose life, for the most part, appears to have been spent in "doing good." "At an early period of it he expressed a wish that he might so live that the blessings of existence should not be thrown away on an idle and useless creature." "From the time that he became independent of his professional occupations, his only thought was, how his zeal and activity could be so applied as to be most conducive to the public good, more particularly as it regarded the lower classes of society. And in all his undertakings, he laid it down as a rule, to put all personal considerations (of difficulty) out of his mind."*

Sir THOS. BERNARD was (with two or three other eminent philanthropists) principally instrumental in establishing the "Society for bettering the Condition of the Poor;" in the progress of which his labours and his writings form a distinguishing feature. His views of rendering permanent benefit to the lower classes of society appear to have been governed by this sound principle, that "*whatever encourages and promotes habits of industry, prudence, forrsight, virtue, and cleanliness among the poor, is beneficial to them and to the country;* and, that whatever removes or diminishes the incitement to any of these qualities is detrimental to the state, and

---

* Life of Sir Thomas Bernard, page 124.

pernicious to the individual. This," he observes, "is the polar star of our benevolent affections; directing them to their true end, and preserving them not only from a capricious selection of objects, which, unjust in principle and injurious in effect, seeks rather to gratify personal whim and distempered humour than to promote the well-being of its fellow-creatures, but also from that indiscriminate and undirected bounty, which may 'give all its goods to feed the poor,' and yet possess no one individual characteristic or property of genuine and useful charity."*

In several parts of his writings Sir THOS. BERNARD expresses his conviction, that the duties of society are of reciprocal and universal obligation; and, that "rank, power, wealth, and influence, constitute no exemption from activity, or attention to duty; but lay a weight of real accumulated responsibility on the possessor." " If [continues he] the poor be *idle* and *vicious*, they are reduced to subsist on the benevolence of the rich: if the rich (I except those to whom health and ability, not will, is wanting) are *selfish, indolent,* and *neglectful* of the *conditions* on which they *hold superiority* of *rank* and *fortune*, they sink into a situation worse than that of being *gratuitously maintained* by *the poor*. They become *paupers of an elevated and distinguished class:* in no way personally contributing to the general stock, but subsisting on the labour of the industrious cottager: and whenever Providence thinks fit to remove such a character, whether in *high* or in *low life*, whether *rich* or *poor*, the community is relieved from an useless burthen."†

This eminent philanthropist was removed from his sphere of active usefulness after a short illness. The fatal event appeared to have been hastened, if not caused, by the extreme exertion which he used in endeavouring to obtain a repeal of the duties on salt; an object which, he was fully convinced, was of the greatest national importance.

But however the conduct of such men may deserve our admiration and esteem, it is not necessary that we possess either eminent talents or great riches to ' do our duty' in that station of life in which Providence has placed us. We may all do something, or contribute something useful to the common stock of society; and if this be ever so little, yet, being done in a spirit of beneficence, according to our means, such offerings of charity will be accepted, like that of the poor widow in the Gospel, who presented *two mites;* of whom our Lord declared, that she had ' cast more in than all they which had cast into the treasury.'

---

* Reports of the " Society for bettering the Condition of the Poor," vol. iii. page 9. Introductory letter.
† Vol. ii. page 27, prefatory introduction.

If pure Christianity really prevailed in the world, instead of the disorders which now afflict and disfigure society, we should behold fruits congenial to its own nature: " love, joy, peace, long-suffering, gentleness, goodness, faith, meekness, temperance; against such there is no law." The beautiful language of the prophet Isaiah would then be realized, " Instead of the thorn shall come up the fir tree, and instead of the brier shall come up the myrtle tree." " For the LORD will comfort Zion: he will comfort all her waste places, and he will make the wilderness like Eden, and her desart like the garden of the LORD; joy and gladness shall be found therein, thanksgiving, and the voice of melody."

FINIS.

SHORTLY WILL BE REPRINTED

(Being the 5th Edition),

FRIENDLY ADVICE,

CONTAINING

MAXIMS OF MORALITY AND PRUDENCE FOR THE CONDUCT OF LIFE:

Addressed to Persons in the lower Stations of Society.

By WILLIAM DAVIS,

One of the Managers of the Bath Provident Institution, or Bank for Savings.

To be had of the same Booksellers; price 4*d.* or 25*s.* per Hundred.

Wood & Co. Printers,
Union-Street, Bath.

ERRATA.

Page 3, line 2, for *have*   read *has.*
     4, —— 9, — *by*   —— *for.*
     5, ——24, — *productions* —— *production.*
    12, —— 4, — *Shcool*   —— *School.*
    23, ——34, — *lesser*   —— *less.*
    25, ——25, — *services*   —— *service.*
    48, ——22, — *Inttitution* —— *Institution.*
    92, 4th line
    fm. bottom — *from*   —— *to.*
   129, —— 2, — *phospate*   —— *phosphate.*
   132, —— 17, — *which last*   —— *the first of which.*

(Continued at back of book)

ISBN 0 7175 0018 7

©

C. A. Burland

1960

First published 1960
Reprinted 1965
Reprinted 1974

HULTON EDUCATIONAL PUBLICATIONS LTD.
Raans Road, Amersham, Bucks.

Printed Offset Litho in Great Britain by
Cox & Wyman Ltd.
London, Fakenham and Reading

For Bryan
as one half of your heritage

Father

Christmas 1982